THE VICTORIAN COOKBOOK

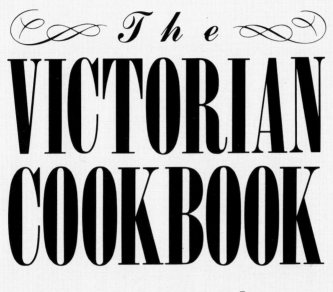

The
VICTORIAN
COOKBOOK

MICHELLE BERRIEDALE-JOHNSON

PHOTOGRAPHY
BY MICHAEL BOYS

INTERLINK BOOKS
NEW YORK

First American edition published 1989 by
INTERLINK BOOKS
An imprint of Interlink Publishing Group, Inc.
99 Seventh Avenue
Brooklyn, New York 11215

Copyright © 1989 Sheldrake Publishing Ltd.
Main text © 1989 Michelle Berriedale-Johnson

Designed and produced by
Sheldrake Press Ltd.
188 Cavendish Road
London SW12 0DA

Library of Congress Cataloging-in-Publication Data

Berriedale-Johnson, Michelle.
   The Victorian cook-book
Michelle Berriedale-Johnson. – 1st American ed.
   p. cm.
   Bibliography: p.
   Includes index.
   ISBN 0-940793-38-5
   1. Cookery, British. 2. Great Britain – Social life
and customs – 19th century. 3. Home economics –
Great Britain – History – 19th century. I. Title.
TX717.B515   1989
641.5941′09′034 – dc20   89-7598   CIP

ISBN 0-940793-38-5

EDITOR: SIMON RIGGE
Managing Editor: Nina Shandloff
Picture Editor: Eleanor Lines
Art Direction and Book Design: Bob Hook
and Ivor Claydon
Photography: Michael Boys, assisted by Liz Gedney
and Alistair Taylor-Young
Food Preparation: Michelle Berriedale-Johnson,
assisted by Jane Suthering and Louise Pickford
Stylist: Helen Payne
Consultants: Anne Cope and Maggie Black
Assistant Editor: Alison Leach
Picture Research: Kathryn Cureton
Editorial Assistant: Helen Ridge
Production: Hugh Allan and Rebecca Bone

Printed in Italy by Imago

ACKNOWLEDGEMENTS

The author gives special thanks to the following for
their contribution to the book: the Brotherton
Library, Leeds, for *The English and Australian
Cookery Book*; Peter Boizot of Kettner's; His Grace
the Late Duke of Northumberland for permission to
use the commonplace book recording the events at
the coming of age of Lord Warkworth; the librarian
of The Reform Club for access to Soyer's cookbooks; Clwyd County Record Office for recipes
from Erddig; Joanne O'Connor of Delmonico's
Restaurant.
Sheldrake Press is grateful also to: Martin Miller, Sue
Greenwood and Philippa Forrest of Chilston Park
for supplying props as well as beautiful surroundings
for the photography sessions; to Sarah Parks Young
of Stanhill Court for putting up with us in her
kitchen and to her daughter, Elinor, for her cheerful
help at all times; to Ian Wallace for his help and
direction in finding suitable locations for the
photography; to Valerie Chandler for the index.

PICTURE CREDITS

The colour photographs in this book were taken by
Michael Boys. We would like to acknowledge the
following sources of the black and white illustrations
which are credited in reading order from the top of
the left-hand column to the bottom of the right-hand
column on every page: Endpapers – Science Museum
London. 20 – The Hulton Deutsch Collection.
21 – Mary Evans Picture Library, The Hulton
Deutsch Collection. 32 – Both from *The Illustrated
London News* 1892 and 1898. 33 – Mary Evans Picture
Library, The Mansell Collection. 37 – *The Modern
Housewife* by Alexis Soyer. 39 – Bottom left, *The
Gastronomic Regenerator* by Alexis Soyer. 49 – The
Mansell Collection, *The Graphic* c.1885. 61 – Top left,
The Graphic 1887. 72 – Both from *Mrs. Beeton's Book
of Household Management* 1898. 73 – Science Museum
London, *Mrs. Beeton's Book of Household
Management* 1898. 85 – Top left, *Sporting and
Dramatic News* c.1885. 96 – Top right, The Hulton
Deutsch Collection. 97 – *The Epicurean* by Charles
Ranhofer 1893. 109 – Both from the commonplace
book of Lord Warkworth's coming of age 1867. 120/
121 – All from The Museum of English Rural Life
University of Reading. 128 – *London Labour and the
London Poor* by Henry Mayhew 1861. 132/133
(upper) – Both from The Museum of English Rural
Life University of Reading. 144 – *Mrs. A.B.
Marshall's Cookery Book* 1887. All other black and
white illustrations are courtesy Dover Publications.

CONTENTS

INTRODUCTION

When I was a small child the Victorian era, that stretched from the eighteen-year-old Queen's accession in 1837 until her death in 1901, was still too recent to be other than generally despised: vulgar, florid, hypocritical, laughable in its foibles and follies. I can remember going with my mother to a rambling old warehouse in south London stacked with unwanted Victorian furniture and artefacts. Beautifully veneered walnut dining tables, that you would be lucky to pick up for $6,000 or $7,000 today, were selling for $50 and $60 alongside button-backed chairs, aspidistra stands and even embroidered silk shawls from the outposts of the Empire – I still have a huge and magnificent black and cream Indian shawl that cost the princely sum of $10.

Now of course tastes have changed and Victorian knick-knacks are pursued with the enthusiasm once reserved for 18th century British silver. The Victorian age was a time of enormous vitality and explosive growth in every field. The population of the British Isles more than doubled between 1800 and 1850 and doubled again by the end of the century; the arrival of steam power transformed transportation and communication in Britain and the United States just as mass production was changing the face of manufacturing industry.

Such violent changes inevitably produced equally violent contrasts in the Victories themselves – from the wealthy industrialist, large-mouthed, large-bellied, beer-swilling and beef-eating, the model for John Bull, to the prudish Queen who insisted on the legs of her chairs being covered with skirts for the sake of propriety. Even in the cooking world such characters appear.

Alexis Soyer, who cooked for the greatest and designed the finest and most modern kitchen in the land, devoted much of his life to setting up soup kitchens to feed the starving poor of Ireland or the malnourished soldiery in the Crimea. Charles Francatelli, who cooked for the Queen, also wrote a *Plain Cookery Book for the Working Classes*. Colonel Kenney Herbert, of the Indian Army, understood the problems of the English "memsahib" far from home and battling with her Indian household so well that he produced a series of excellent cookbooks to assist her.

As for Victorian women, fictional ladies may have simpered and had frequent recourse to the smelling salts, but real life ladies could be eminently practical. Isabella Beeton sat up till midnight in her husband's office editing her magazine; Florence Nightingale rode with Soyer round the battlefields of Sebastopol planning their new hospital kitchens, and Eliza Acton campaigned vigorously to improve the quality of food as an essential element of good health.

As a result Victorian cooking is not nearly as complicated as one might imagine. Of course, there are some long, involved and labor-intensive recipes, especially from the great chefs who had endless resources of both food and manpower. But many of the dishes to be found, for example, in the works of Mrs. Beeton, Eliza Acton, Dr. Kitchiner or Fannie Farmer are surprisingly simple, relying on long slow cooking to achieve their really excellent flavor.

The business of writing a "receipt" was considerably less haphazard in the 19th century than it had been in earlier times, when very few cooks could read or write. Ingredients were then so severely restricted by season and location that every possibility was given, leaving the cook to use whichever was available. However, even in the 19th century, food writing was by no means the accurate science that it is – or at least should be – today. Ingredients and method were seldom separated in a recipe. Eliza Acton in the 1840s was the pioneer in this respect, listing her ingredients separately and accurately. Isabella Beeton, twenty years later, did the same, adding cooking times, the number of people the dish should feed and seasonality for good measure. And by the end of the century Fannie Farmer was insisting that tablespoonfuls be specified as level or heaped and not left to the inclination of the cook. But they were in the minority; Francatelli, Soyer and Dr. Kitchiner in England, and Eliza Leslie, Marian Harland and

Catherine Beecher in the United States left many such details to the reader's ingenuity.

Equally, recipes were frequently merely copied from another cookbook with no attempt at accreditation – as is still all too often the case. The highly successful Farmer edition of the *Boston Cooking School Cookbook*, for example, incorporated most of Mrs. Lincoln's recipes from the earlier edition with never a mention of who originally devised them. To be fair, Fannie Farmer did revise most of the recipes that she "borrowed," as did the majority of the other cooks featured in this book, but beware if you wish to venture further afield into Victorian cooking.

The charge most often leveled at 19th century cooks the world over is one of extravagance, especially in their use of dairy products – butter, cream and eggs. Although a 19th century diet was by no means ideal – people tended to eat too much in any case – its high fat content could be better justified in their time than in ours. Their houses were drafty and all too often unheated so that warmth had to be generated from within – a job that fat does very efficiently. The lack of automobiles, elevators, buses and trains meant that even the wealthy had to take more exercise than most of us do today – another good way to use up high calorie fats. In the 19th century food was also less processed and richer in fiber than ours; as a result less of the fat was absorbed as it passed through the system. And anyhow, our great grandparents simply enjoyed the taste of butter and cream!

It has also to be remembered that the average middle-class household a hundred years ago was much larger than is usual today. In England an average family might include five or six children and have three to ten staff; in America there might be even more children although usually rather fewer staff. But in any case, catering for ten or twelve people meant that large roasts of meat were very practical. The difficulty of daily shopping (no supermarkets open day and night, seven days a week) and the fact that the only cool place for storing fresh food was the larder – fine in winter but not much use in summer – meant that it was necessary to prepare food that would "last." So again it made sense to buy a large piece of meat, served as a roast on the

first day, eaten cold on the second and then turned into pies, hashes and curries, all of which keep well, until the cook had another chance to buy fresh supplies.

The whole social ethos surrounding food preparation and service has also changed dramatically in the last hundred years, although not in exactly the same way on both sides of the Atlantic. In England in Victorian times, only the poorest would expect to have to survive without a servant, and much of an aspiring Victorian lady's social standing depended on how many she employed. Any Englishwoman, therefore, who bought a cookbook did so for the purpose of instructing her cook rather than with the idea of making a dish herself. In the United States servants were less common, except in the Deep South, so the average Northern or Western middle-class woman of the house did much of the daily food preparation herself. On the other hand, an immensely rigid and complicated code of eating and mealtime etiquette grew up as a measure of refinement and social status. The poor on both sides of the Atlantic cooked what food they could afford on the basis of habit and tradition, with little recourse to cookbooks.

The arrival of rail transportation increased enormously the range of ingredients available to the 19th century cook although much food, especially in the countryside, was still grown or made at home and was, therefore, totally seasonal. Whatever else was needed was bought from itinerant salesmen, at the weekly or monthly markets in the local towns, or from small specialist providers such as butchers, fishmongers and grocers.

Lack of refrigeration meant that food still had a very short shelflife. Fish, meat and dairy products, for example, could not be expected to last more than a couple of days in a store or on a stall – although all kinds of ruses were employed by dishonest storekeepers to sell off rotten food. By the 1870s (the 1880s and 1890s in England) canned meats, fish and vegetables and ready-made jellies and preserves could be purchased to supplement seasonal and locally grown food. By the end of the century, aided by efficient rail transportation and refrigeration, massive food processing industries – such as meat packing in Chicago –

had developed.

In terms of quality, taste and texture, 19th century foodstuffs do not equate with today's. Horticulture and agriculture had become recognized sciences in the 1700s, but even by the 1850s they had done relatively little to change the "natural" taste and texture of food. Far from trying to standardize his produce, the 19th century grower gloried in the number of varieties of fruit and vegetables he could produce – thirty or forty types of apples and pears were regularly marketed in different parts of the country. Throughout the century research continued into improving taste, texture and appearance, but it was not until the second half of the 20th century that uniformity of color and form outstripped flavor as the prime goal of the grower. Only in the last decades of the 19th century did the use of chemical fertilizers become widespread; the majority of 19th century food was grown with only the help of traditional animal fertilizers. The closest approximation today to the taste of fresh 19th century produce is organically grown or reared fruit, vegetables or meats.

Another food dramatically affected by industrialization was bread. Until the 1880s wheat was milled between two stones. This produced a relatively coarse, light brown flour with the wheat germ still intact. For centuries the ambition of bakers had been to produce pure white bread, despite the constant complaints of cooks and nutritionists – Eliza Acton was only one in a long line – that coarse brown bread was much better for the digestive system. The millers removed as many of the imperfections as possible from the flour by sifting, but even so, the whitest bread was only the equivalent of a very pale modern whole-wheat loaf. Then in the 1880s came the roller mill. This acted as a monster mangle, crushing the wheat germ between its rollers and allowing the miller access to the pure white starch in the middle. This not only produced a genuine white flour but, with the disposal of the perishable wheat germ, gave it a much longer shelflife.

Nineteenth century kitchens, picturesque though they may be, leave much to be desired as far as the modern cook is concerned. Nonetheless, the coal-fired range, which was to be found in almost every household by the end

of the century, was a dramatic improvement on the open fire and the old brick or iron hobs. But by modern standards, the range was extremely dirty, unreliable and almost uncontrolable. There was no way of adjusting the heat of either the hot plates or the oven, except by increasing or reducing the draft and thereby the speed at which the fire burned. Inevitably, cooking temperatures were a much more erratic affair than they are today.

By the 19th century scales were also commonplace, so ingredients could be weighed with accuracy. Clocks were to be found in every kitchen and could be read by almost every cook (not the case a couple of centuries earlier) so timing could also be relatively exact. Although gadgets such as grinders were proliferating toward the end of the century, those workhorses of the modern kitchen – the electric mixer, blender and food processor – were of course unknown to the Victorian cook. This meant that all beating (one cake recipe calls for four hours' worth) had to be done by hand, as did chopping, pasting (through a hair strainer) and most grinding or pounding (with a mortar and pestle). Fortunately, most Victorian cooks did at least have plenty of spare hands.

My choice of writers and chefs to include in this book has had to be arbitrary – there are many, many more whose books are well worth reading and whose food is well worth cooking. However, I have tried to choose characters and situations that would give the broadest picture of the richness and diversity of 19th century society. To provide a more comprehensive social background so essential for understanding the eating habits of any country or period, there are also short features between the chapters describing a variety of topics from drinking to food adulteration, from servants and kitchen design to eating out in private clubs and restaurants.

For anyone who is interested in pursuing the subject further, I have included a bibliography at the end of the book. But be warned: many of the books listed are long since out of print and will only be found in a few libraries, or possibly a secondhand bookstore

Following the recipes in this book should not present any problems to a modern cook. The more complicated ones may involve a number of different processes but none is particularly difficult to achieve. I have given quantities for serving numbers which seemed appropriate to each cook. I could not, for example, imagine anyone serving an eight or nine course Francatelli or Soyer dinner to a party of three so, in those chapters, the recipes serve eight or ten people. On the same basis, the recipes derived from the more homely cooks are for four or six people. Where a dish is to be served as part of a long and elaborate meal, I have usually suggested quantities that will allow your guests to sample each course without having to be helped from the table – for example, a dish may serve four as a main course or eight as part of the complete meal. Incidentally, all spoon measurements are level unless "heaped" is specified.

I tested the recipes by giving dinner parties, the idea being to serve the dishes in as similar circumstances as possible to the original. This sometimes involved serving up to nine dishes for one dinner, which I have to admit daunted even me. However, since so many of the dishes needed to be cooked in advance, I found that with the judicious use of a microwave and a

couple of ovens for holding or reheating it proved remarkably easy to do. Indeed, in most cases I found myself cooking, serving and clearing a whole meal for eight to ten guests with no assistance at all – and very little hassle.

So please do not be put off by any apparent complexity. Do not, either, be put off – or let your guests be put off – by the seemingly lavish food. The quantities given should enable everyone to enjoy a small portion of each dish and, hopefully, leave you some good pickings for the next day as well!

Finally, a brief but heartfelt word of thanks to Alison Leach who edited the book so ably, to Eleanor Lines, Nina Shandloff and Bob Hook of Sheldrake Press who have done such a splendid job of designing and producing it, and to Michael Boys whose photographs capture the spirit of the cooks and their recipes so perfectly.

I hope you enjoy making the dishes as much as I have and that they will tempt you to investigate further the cooking of the past.

Michelle Berriedale-Johnson
London, February 1989

CHAPTER ONE

A WINTER BANQUET WITH CHARLES FRANCATELLI

For a man who was to become chef to Queen Victoria, remarkably little is known about Charles Elmé Francatelli. He was born in 1805 and was English, though presumably of Italian or French parentage. He learned his trade in France and claimed to have worked under the great Carême, thus making himself a rarity among early 19th century chefs: an Englishman who had genuinely trained in France. He was attractive looking (to judge by the engraving in the front of his book, *The Modern Cook*) and probably personable. He married a lady called Elizabeth, wrote four cookbooks and died in Eastbourne on August 10, 1876. His professional life is scarcely any better documented.

Success appears to have come early. By the time Francatelli entered the Queen's service in 1840 or 1841, he had already held four important posts in private households and spent a brief period at Crockford's, the enormously successful gambling club. His first appointment seems to have been with the young Earl of Chesterfield, followed by spells in the households of Viscount Ednam of Ednam, the Earl of Dudley and the young Scottish Baron Kinnaird. Lord Kinnaird, the son of a notoriously stingy father, was intent on becoming a "distinguished bon vivant" – an aspiration no doubt much to Francatelli's taste.

On leaving Lord Kinnaird's employ in 1840 Francatelli went to Crockford's, which had been established in 1827 by William Crockford, an astute Cockney fishmonger. The secret of Crockford's success, apart from its plush sur-

roundings, was the excellence of the food and drink that was offered free to its patrons. The responsibility for the kitchens had rested with Eustache Ude, a flamboyant French chef whom William Crockford considered so important to the club that he paid him a salary of over £1,000 a year. By 1840 Ude's success had gone to his head and Crockford was forced to replace him. The choice fell, flatteringly, on Francatelli but the appointment was not a success. Despite his undoubted talents, Francatelli was unable to step into the shoes that Ude had filled so amply. However, in the short time that he spent at the club, he caught the eye of the Earl of Erroll, Queen Victoria's Lord Steward of the Household, who asked him to cook for the royal family.

Although Francatelli spent less than a year in the royal service, he unquestionably saw it as the high point in his career. The Queen was still young and fun-loving and his brief was wide. Dinners normally ran to twenty or thirty dishes and were served in two courses or services. The first consisted of two or three soups, two or three fish dishes and two to four "removes" or *relevés*. The latter were usually meat dishes, sometimes roast, sometimes "made up," which formed a bridge between the soup and fish dishes and the entrées. The entrées, generally about four of them, were "made up" dishes of meat, poultry or game interspersed with the occasional vegetable. The second course consisted of two to four roasts followed by more "removes," but this time these were mainly sweet dishes: "puddings," soufflés and so forth. At this point recourse could also be had to the sideboard which was kept laden with cold roasts and side dishes. The *entremets* that came at the end of the meal were a collection of up to fifteen vegetable and sweet

OPPOSITE: JOHN DORY WITH DUTCH SAUCE AND PUREE OF CARROTS A LA CRECY

dishes with the occasional fish dish also appearing at more lavish dinners.

Such meals, prepared by a staff of twenty-four cooks and two "Yeomen of the Kitchen" or deputy chefs in addition to Francatelli, obviously allowed the chef to indulge himself to the full. This Francatelli certainly did, sparing neither ingredients nor time in the preparation of his dishes. It was probably this very lavishness which truncated his career as royal chef, his appointment coinciding with one of Prince Albert's drives for economy and "the simple life."

After his royal service Francatelli worked in several other noble households, spent seven years in the 1850s at the Reform Club to which Alexis Soyer had lent such glamour in the previous decade, managed the St. James's Hotel in Berkeley Street and finally managed the Free Mason's Tavern in Great Queen Street. He also wrote his four cookbooks:

The Modern Cook (from which the menu at right is quoted), first published in 1846 and which went into many "editions."

A Plain Cookery Book for the Working Classes, published in 1852 in an attempt, maybe, to rebut accusations over the extravagance of his cooking; in later years he was said to claim that he could feed a thousand families on the food that was wasted in London every day.

The Good Cook's Guide and Butler's Assistant, published in 1861.

The Royal English and Foreign Confectionery Book, published in 1862.

Francatelli's cooking was definitely in the tradition of French *haute cuisine:* complex liaisons and sauces, stock and glazes, pastries and soufflés. Unlike Carême he was not particularly interested in garnish or in creating the stunning *pièces montées* that were such a feature of early 19th century cooking. Indeed, his decoration was seldom inspired and quite often perfunctory. But his recipes, although not as detailed in terms of weights and measures as Eliza Acton's for example, are easy to follow and reliable.

The menu reproduced here is for a "Dinner for Twelve Persons in January." It shows a happy disregard for linguistic purity – and makes one shudder at the thought of the indigestion that must have followed such a meal. I have chosen nine dishes from the menu that, with perseverance, a 20th century diner should be able to get through without any too disastrous results.

Dinner for twelve persons – January

FIRST COURSE

Soups

Macaroni clear soup
Purée of carrots à la Crécy

Fishes

Fillets of whiting à la Royale
(whiting marinated in vinaigrette, deep fried in batter and served with butter sauce)
John Dory with Dutch sauce

Removes

Braised beef à la Polonaise aux choux rouges
Poularde à la Périgeux
(chicken in truffle sauce)

Entrées

Boudins of pheasant à la Reine
(minced pheasant sausages)
Fillets of pigeon à la duxelle
Mutton cutlets, à la Bourguignotte
Marrow patties with fine herbs

SECOND COURSE

Roasts

Teal
(small freshwater duck)
Hare

Removes

Brown bread soufflé
Ramequins à la Sefton
(eggs, cheese and bread crumbs baked in individual molds)

Entremets

Salsifis à la crème
Vol-au-vent of greengages
Potatoes au gratin
(potatoes baked with eggs and cream)
Noyeau cream
Lemon jelly
Pithiviers cake

PUREE OF CARROTS A LA CRECY

Serves 8

This is one of the thirty-two "Purées of Vegetables in General for Soups" in *The Modern Cook*. These include everything from homely split peas to luxurious chestnuts and asparagus. You can make the carrot soup in advance and freeze it.

INGREDIENTS

4½ cups roughly chopped old carrots
2 celery stalks, roughly chopped
1 large onion, roughly chopped
6 tablespoons butter
about 1½ teaspoons sugar
salt and white pepper
2 quarts good chicken stock

Put the carrots, celery and onion into a pan, cover with boiling water, bring back to a boil and simmer for 10 minutes. Drain the vegetables. Put 4 tablespoons of the butter in the pan with 1 teaspoon of the sugar and a little salt. Add the vegetables and cook very gently for 30 minutes. Add the chicken stock, bring to a boil and simmer for 1 hour.

Purée the soup in a blender or processor and then rub through a strainer. Return the purée to the pan, add the remaining butter and sugar, salt and pepper to taste.

You can serve the soup as it is or garnished with a little finely chopped parsley or a teaspoon of whipped cream.

JOHN DORY WITH DUTCH SAUCE

Serves 8 as an appetizer, 4 as a main course

John Dory or St. Pierre is a delicious Mediterranean fish, but it is both expensive and difficult to obtain; if you cannot find any, substitute fillets of halibut or sole. Francatelli says of John Dory that "this kind of fish, although a great favourite with many, is very seldom sent to table in any other shape than as a plain boiled fish, either with Lobster or Dutch sauce." I think it kinder to the fish to steam it. The Dutch sauce is, logically, very similar to a Hollandaise, but less temperamental.

INGREDIENTS

8 fillets of John Dory, skinned but with
   the skins retained if possible
1 lemon, thinly sliced
½ cup dry white wine
4 medium egg yolks
1 stick butter, cut into small pieces
2–3 tablespoons béchamel sauce (page
   145)
salt and white pepper
pinch of nutmeg
8 lemon twists or butterflies for garnish

Note If you are presenting the complete menu, you will also need béchamel sauce for the salsify.

Roll up the fillets of fish and lay the rolls in the top of a steamer. Put the fish skins, if you have them, in the bottom of the steamer with the wine, lemon and 1¼-2½ cups water, depending on the size of your pan. Steam the fish for 10 minutes, or until it is cooked.

Meanwhile put the egg yolks in a heavy pan or the top of a double boiler, with the butter, 2 tablespoons of the béchamel sauce and a little salt, pepper and nutmeg. Heat very gently, stirring continuously until the sauce "assumes a smooth compact body" or thickens slightly into a cream; remove from the heat immediately. If the sauce shows any sign of curdling, add the remaining tablespoon of béchamel and stir vigorously. (Francatelli then strained his sauce, but I did not find that necessary.)

Lay a rolled fish fillet on each plate, spoon over a ladleful of sauce, garnish with the lemon twists or butterflies and serve immediately.

BRAISED BEEF A LA POLONAISE AUX CHOUX ROUGES

Serves 8 to 10

The original of this recipe calls for a 20 lb piece of beef and includes a Poivrade sauce. I found that the sauce masked the delicious flavors of the cooking juices and beets, but I have included the recipe for those who wish to use it. I have also reduced the quantities of beef to more manageable proportions. Although the dish was intended to be served hot, it is just as good cold.

INGREDIENTS

2½ lb top round of beef, in one piece
¼ lb fatty bacon, cut in thin strips
some beef bones, if available, broken
    to allow the marrow to escape
1 medium carrot, chopped
2 celery stalks, chopped
2 small onions, stuck all over with
    cloves
generous bunch of herbs (including
    parsley stalks, thyme and bay leaves)
    or 2 bouquets garnis
about 10 black peppercorns
⅓ cup brandy
1¼ cups medium sweet sherry
good beef stock or a combination of
    good beef consommé and water
1 cup finely diced raw beets
salt and freshly ground black pepper

Cut the beef horizontally into three thick "slices," cover each "slice" with a layer of the bacon, reassemble the joint and secure it neatly with string. Place the bones, carrot, celery, onions, herbs and peppercorns in the bottom of a flameproof casserole just large enough to hold the beef. Add the brandy and sherry and bring to a boil. Lower in the beef and add sufficient stock or consommé mixture to cover the meat. Cover the casserole, bring it to a boil slowly and simmer it very gently for about 2½ hours. A sharp knife should be able to slide into the meat encountering no resistance. Cool the meat in its juices.

When the meat is cold, skim any fat from the top of the pan, then remove the meat and dry it with paper towels. Strain 3¾ cups of the stock juices into a pan and add the diced beets. Bring to a boil and boil briskly until the beets are cooked

and the stock is reduced to 2½ cups – about 20 minutes. Season to taste with salt and pepper.

To serve hot, return the meat to the pan and re-heat very gently in the juices. Serve sliced, on a bed of cabbage (see opposite) with the beets and juices spooned over and accompanied by the Poivrade sauce if you wish (see below).

POIVRADE SAUCE

INGREDIENTS

1 tablespoon butter
2 carrots, finely chopped
2 medium onions, finely chopped
4 celery stalks, finely chopped
4 slices of lean bacon or 2 thin slices of
    ham, finely chopped
2 bay leaves, 2 sprigs of thyme and a
    handful of parsley, or 3 bouquets
    garnis
2 cups medium sherry
1 cup white wine vinegar
peppercorns
3 blades of mace or generous pinch of
    ground mace
2½ cups good beef consommé
½ cup good brown sauce (page 145) or
    gravy, if available

Melt the butter in a heavy pan and fry the carrot, onion, celery, bacon and fresh herbs gently for about 15 minutes, or until they are lightly browned but not burned. Add the sherry and vinegar with a few peppercorns, the mace and bouquets garnis if you are using them instead of the fresh herbs. Bring to a boil and boil briskly for 10 minutes to reduce substantially. Add the consommé and brown sauce and cook for a further 5 minutes. Pass through a fine strainer and adjust the seasoning to taste before serving.

Braised Beef a la Polonaise aux Choux Rouges with Poivrade Sauce and Puree of Carrots a la Crecy

CHOUX ROUGES

INGREDIENTS

3 tablespoons olive oil
2 lb red cabbage, thinly sliced
1 large cooking apple or 2 large, tart
   eating apples, peeled and cubed
2 tablespoons red wine vinegar
¾ cup beef stock
salt and pepper

Heat the oil in a large pan, add the cabbage, stir well, cover and sweat gently for 10 minutes. Add the apple, vinegar and stock, cover and sweat for a further 10 minutes, or until the cabbage is cooked but still slightly crunchy. Season to taste with salt and pepper. Serve warm or cold.

FILLETS OF PIGEON A LA DUXELLE

Serves 8 as part of the complete menu, 4 as a main course

The original recipe for duxelle sauce includes chopped truffles that would no doubt be delicious but would make the dish extortionately expensive – by all means include them if cost is no object! Francatelli also assumes that every kitchen will have a constant supply of brown and white sauces. If you are following the whole menu, you will also need béchamel sauce for the fish and the salsify; if you are just making the pigeon dish and do not wish to have to make a sauce in order to make a sauce, substitute heavy cream. You can make the duxelle sauce in advance and reheat it carefully to serve.

INGREDIENTS

2-4 tablespoons butter
1½ cups finely chopped mushroom
2 slices of fatty bacon, very finely chopped
4 shallots, very finely chopped
1¼ cups dryish white French wine
⅓ cup very finely chopped truffles (optional)
good handful of parsley, finely chopped
salt and pepper
generous pinch of nutmeg
⅓ cup béchamel sauce (page 145) or heavy cream
4 medium egg yolks
juice of ½–1 lemon
8 pigeon or squab breasts
1 egg, beaten
couple of handfuls of fresh brown bread crumbs

Note You will probably have to buy whole pigeons or squab and remove the breasts.

To prepare the sauce, melt 1 tablespoon of the butter in a heavy pan and add the mushrooms, bacon and shallots. Cover the pan and sweat gently for 10 minutes. Meanwhile reduce the wine by boiling it rapidly for 5 minutes. Add the truffles, if you are using them, parsley, seasoning and wine to the mushrooms and cook them for a further 5 minutes. Remove from the heat and add the béchamel sauce or cream and the egg yolks;

stir well. Add lemon juice to taste and adjust the seasoning if necessary. Keep hot, but do not boil or the sauce may curdle.

Dry the pigeon or squab breasts thoroughly, then coat lightly in egg and bread crumbs. Fry them gently in the remaining butter for 4 to 5 minutes on each side, or until they are lightly browned and cooked through. Serve individually or on a dish with the sauce.

MUTTON CUTLETS A LA BOURGUIGNOTTE

Serves 8 as part of the complete menu, 4 as a main course

Francatelli uses mutton cutlets, but since these are now hard to find, lamb can happily be substituted. It is better to make the quenelles a few hours before you need them as they are easier to handle when well chilled. You can also cook the cutlets in advance; when you are ready to serve, warm them through in the sauce and finish the dish as described.

QUENELLES

INGREDIENTS

3 large, thick slices of good quality white bread, crusts removed
4 tablespoons butter
2 tablespoons chicken stock or dry white wine
3 medium egg yolks
salt and white pepper

Put the bread into a bowl and cover it with tepid water. Leave to soak for 10 to 15 minutes, then squeeze it out thoroughly in a clean dish towel. Put the bread into a pan with the butter and stock or wine and cook gently, stirring continuously with a wooden spoon until it "assumes the appearance of paste and no longer adheres to the bottom of the pan." Remove the pan from the heat, add the egg yolks and a generous seasoning of salt and pepper and stir vigorously to amalgamate the mixture. Form it into little quenelles with a teaspoon and place on an oiled baking sheet or dish. Cover the quenelles and chill them in the refrigerator for 2 hours.

CUTLETS

INGREDIENTS

2½ tablespoons butter
½ lb small white onions
8 mutton or lamb cutlets, trimmed
1½ cups fairly finely chopped
  mushroom caps
1¾ cups reasonable claret
salt and pepper
generous pinch of nutmeg
1 teaspoon sugar
¼ cup brown sauce, consommé or stock

Melt about 1½ teaspoons of the butter in a pan and fry the onions gently until they are lightly browned and nearly cooked. Melt the remaining butter in a large heavy sauté or frying pan. Fry the cutlets briskly on both sides until they are nicely colored; pour off any excess fat. Add the mushrooms and onions, 1¼ cups of the red wine, the seasoning and sugar. Make sure that the mushrooms are at least coated in the liquid. Cover the pan and simmer gently for 20 minutes, or until the cutlets are cooked.

Remove the cutlets with a perforated spoon, arrange them around the outside of a heated serving dish and keep warm. Add the brown sauce, consommé or stock to the pan with the remaining wine; cook for 2 minutes. Add the quenelles to the pan carefully and simmer for a further 4 minutes, or until the quenelles are cooked. Spoon the quenelles, mushrooms, onions and sauce into the middle of the serving dish and over the cutlets and serve immediately.

SALSIFIS A LA CREME
Serves 8

The salsify can be prepared in advance and reheated gently in the sauce; a microwave is ideal, and it would need about 2 minutes. Francatelli places "some croûtons of fried bread or fleurons around the dish to serve," but I do not feel that is necessary unless you are feeling very energetic.

INGREDIENTS

10 salsify roots, peeled
juice of 1 lemon
1½ teaspoons butter
3–4 tablespoons béchamel sauce (page
  145)
salt and pepper

Cut the salsify into 1 inch lengths and leave in cold water to cover, with a squeeze of lemon juice to keep it white, until you are ready to cook it. Turn the salsify with its acidulated water into a pan, bring to a boil and simmer until cooked but not mushy – about 10 minutes. Drain the salsify and return to the pan with the butter, béchamel sauce and a little salt and pepper. Reheat the salsify in the sauce before serving and add more salt, pepper and lemon juice if you think they are needed.

PITHIVIERS CAKE

Serves 8 to 10

Francatelli uses whole almonds that have to be laboriously pounded with white of egg; using ground almonds takes a lot of the hard work out of the cake. You can also use a good quality, ready-made puff pastry if you do not want to embark on making your own. The cake can be made in advance and kept for several days.

INGREDIENTS

1¾ cups ground almonds
½ cup extra-fine sugar
½ cup crumbled ratafias (small
*   macaroons can be substituted)*
½ cup butter, softened
4 medium egg yolks
2 tablespoons orange flower water
puff pastry for 7-inch 2-crust pie
extra-fine sugar for sprinkling

In a food processor or mixer beat the almonds, sugar, ratafias, butter, egg yolks and orange flower water until you have "a soft, creamy paste." If it seems too solid, add a little more orange flower water.

Divide the pastry in half and roll out one portion large enough to line a 7 inch pie plate. Fill it with the almond cream and smooth the surface. Fold the edges of the pastry down on to the filling and moisten this rim. Roll out the remaining pastry and cover the almond cream. Use the trimmings to decorate the top of the cake. Sprinkle lightly with sugar and bake at 300° for 40 minutes. Allow the cake to cool completely before removing it from the pan and serving.

NOYEAU CREAM

Serves 8

The basic Bavarian cream can be flavored with almost anything you like: orange, lemon, vanilla, rose water, Maraschino or essence of almonds. The flavoring used in Noyeau Cream is almonds, and I found that Amaretto was particularly successful.

INGREDIENTS

¼ cup extra-fine sugar
2½ cups heavy cream
1 envelope gelatin
juice of 1–2 lemons
⅓ cup Amaretto

Add the sugar to the cream and whip very lightly with a balloon whisk until it is just starting to thicken: it is very easy to overwhip. Meanwhile, soften and melt the gelatin in the juice of 1 lemon in a small bowl standing in a pan of boiling water. Cool the gelatin and add the Amaretto to it. When it is quite cool stir it carefully into the cream mixture with a little more lemon juice if you think it needs it.

Oil a fluted or ring mold with almond oil (if you cannot get this, good quality sunflower oil is almost flavorless) and pour in the cream mixture. Chill in a refrigerator until set. Loosen the edges of the cream with a knife and unmold very carefully on to a decorative serving dish. If you are nervous, you can set the cream in a decorative bowl or soufflé dish and serve from this. You can either serve the cream plain or decorate it with candied violets or roses; if you have made it in a ring mold, you could fill the center with ratafia or other small dessert cookies.

BROWN BREAD SOUFFLE

Serves 8

Although Francatelli calls this dessert a soufflé, it contains such a large proportion of bread crumbs that it scarcely rises at all; its consistency is more like a light steamed pudding. It is, however, quite delicious. You can prepare the mixture in advance and leave it in the refrigerator for several hours before cooking it.

NOYEAU CREAM (LEFT) WITH RATAFIA COOKIES AND BROWN
BREAD SOUFFLE WITH CREAM

INGREDIENTS

3¾ cups fresh brown bread crumbs
1¼ cups heavy cream
½ cup extra-fine sugar
4 tablespoons butter
1 teaspoon ground cinnamon
juice of 1 lemon
5 medium large eggs, separated

Put the bread crumbs in a fairly large pan with the cream, sugar, butter, cinnamon and lemon juice and heat gently until the butter has melted. Stir the mixture until the ingredients are thoroughly amalgamated. Remove the pan from the heat and add the egg yolks; mix thoroughly. Whip the egg whites until they hold their shape in soft peaks. Stir one third of the egg white into the bread crumb mixture gently to lighten it, then fold in the remainder. Spoon the mixture into a buttered soufflé dish – it should come three quarters of the way up the sides – and bake at 350° for 30 minutes. Remove from the oven and serve warm, with or without extra cream.

— 19 —

VICTORIAN SERVANTS

Victorian England was, indubitably, the age of the servant. In an era of vigorous social climbing servants conveyed status in a way that could not be achieved by any other means. So one servant, at the very least, was obligatory as you started your struggle up society's ladder. It was not a totally one-sided bargain. Domestic service may have been badly paid and involved long hours, but it guaranteed poor girls a roof over their heads, security and, at least in the larger households, plenty of food.

In the 18th century servants had also been used as status symbols, but then they were usually male, handsomely attired in fancy liveries. Women went into service too, but they were un-liveried and remained in the background. The change came with the imposition of a "luxury" servants' tax on all male servants (in 1853 it was twenty-one shillings per annum for men over eighteen and ten shillings and sixpence for boys; in 1869 it was altered to fifteen shillings for all male servants and it remained this until the tax was finally abolished in 1937). This resulted in a rapid switch to female domestic servants, although men continued to dominate the coach house and gardens. Toward the end of the century there were nearly three times as many female domestic servants as male, constituting 12.8% of the total female population in 1871. Moreover, for most of the century, at least one third of the female servants were aged between fifteen and twenty, some starting work as young as eight.

The majority of girls hoping to go into service came from the country and ended up in one of the big cities, where the demand was insatiable. They might have done some part-time "daily" cleaning in their home village (the wages helping to buy the "uniform" they would need for their first job) but many would have had little training apart from what they had received at home. "Places" were found through word of mouth or recommendation, advertisements or sometimes an agency or a "mop fair." Once the girl had secured a post, her future life depended entirely on the sort of household she had joined.

The worst off were the "maids of all work" or general servants who were to be found only in

A GROUP OF HOUSEMAIDS IN 1892, ONE HOLDING A HOT WATER CAN

the smallest households. With the occasional assistance of a part-time "girl" they were expected to clean, cook for and entirely maintain the family. Their duties included making the beds, emptying the slop buckets, scrubbing the steps, blacking the grates and making up the fires, cooking, laying the table, serving meals to both the family and any temporary servants, and washing up. It was hardly surprising that they needed to be up at 6:30 am and seldom got back to bed before 11 pm. In return they could expect to be paid between £5 and £10 per year, to be given two weeks' vacation, with maybe a half-day on Sunday and another evening off. They would also get their room and board although the room was seldom more than spartan. Of course their lot depended greatly on the family for whom they worked and though there are various hideous tales of servant maltreatment, these are balanced by other stories of excellent and mutually beneficial relations between mistress and maid.

As the family moved up in the world, so its servants increased. *Mrs. Beeton's Book of Household Management*, published in 1861, gives the following table showing the number of domestics that a family's income should allow:
£200 per year – a maid of all work and an occasional girl
£300 per year – a maid of all work and a nurse-maid

£500 per year – a cook, a housemaid and a nurse-maid

£750 per year – a cook, a housemaid, a nursemaid and a footboy

£1,000 per year – a cook, an upper housemaid, a nursemaid, an under housemaid and a male servant.

In larger and wealthier families, the servant population could run into hundreds, when they formed a society entirely of their own, the lower echelons having no contact whatever with the families they served. Indeed, in a large house, the family would never expect to see a maid at work; the cleaning of the downstairs rooms had to be finished before the family came down to breakfast, the bedrooms were cleaned during the day, and any other necessary tasks had to be fitted into times when the family or its guests were otherwise occupied.

If the social hierarchy was strict above stairs, it was doubly so below them. In the greatest houses a male steward was employed on whose shoulders rested the total running of the house. However, the majority of well-to-do families employed a housekeeper, whose responsibilities were seldom lighter. If a butler was also employed, he was in charge of the male staff, the housekeeper of the female; if there was no butler, she ruled alone. The housekeeper was always addressed by the courtesy title of Mrs., by family and servants alike, whether she was married or not.

Next in status were the lady's maid and the

PREPARING A MEAL FOR A VICTORIAN FAMILY AT THE TURN OF THE CENTURY

valet. They alone were appointed or dismissed by the master or mistress of the house (the housekeeper or butler engaged all other servants). Because of their specially intimate relationship with their employers, they held envied positions in the hierarchy, but were often disliked for being overbearing and superior. Level pegging with them was the cook, whose word was law in anything relating to the kitchen. In a house with children, the head nurse or "nanny" was also regarded as one of the upper servants, but she held an uncomfortable position midway between the servants' hall and the drawing-room.

If the household were large enough to have its

DOMESTIC STAFF OF A MID 19TH CENTURY HOUSEHOLD

---

own laundry (most large houses, where up to a thousand napkins could be used in a week, had a complete laundry department), the senior laundry maid would also count among the "top ten" servants while the rest would be made up by upper housemaids. These "top ten" ate in the housekeeper's room (with the exception of the head nurse who normally had her meals in the nursery with the children) and were treated with as much respect by the other servants as the master or mistress themselves. Although discipline was strict there was plenty of good fellowship among the lower servants and despite the hard work, long hours and stringent rules, the position of a servant in a big household was much to be desired.

CHAPTER TWO

DINNER
WITH THE REDOUBTABLE
DR. KITCHINER

Dr. William Kitchiner, self-styled "M.D.," died in 1827, ten years before Queen Victoria came to the throne, but his book, *The Cook's Oracle; containing Receipts for Plain Cookery on the most Economical Plan for Private Families*, continued to be popular throughout much of her reign. It went through many editions and in 1861 was paraphrased and republished as the *Shilling Kitchiner*. As late as 1866 William Jerdan included the doctor and a description of his dinners, in his collection of biographical essays, *Men I Have Known*.

The writer of a long obituary in the *Gentleman's Magazine* quotes the invitation to one of these dinners which ran as follows:

Dear Sir,
The honour of your company is requested to dine with the Committee of Taste on Wednesday next 10th inst. The specimens will be placed on the table at 5 o'clock precisely, when the business of the day will immediately commence. I have the honour to be your most obedient servant,
William Kitchiner, Secretary
25th August 1825

43, Warren Street,
Fitzroy Square.

At the last general meeting it was unanimously resolved that

1st. An invitation to the Eta Beta Pi must be answered in writing as soon as possible after it is received, within 24 hours at the latest reckoning from that on which it was dated; otherwise the Secretary will have the profound regret to feel that the invitation has been definitely declined.

2nd. The Secretary, having represented that the perfection of several of the preparations is so exquisitely evanescent, that the delay of one minute after their arrival at the meridian of concoction will render them no longer worthy of men of taste. Therefore, to ensure the punctual attendance of those illustrious gastrophilists, who on grand occasions are invited to join this high tribunal of taste for their own pleasure and the benefit of their company, it is irrevocably resolved that the janitor be ordered not to admit any visitor, of whatever eminence or appetite, after the hour which the Secretary will have announced the specimens are ready.

By order of the Committee,
William Kitchiner, Secretary.

These dinners and the small group of regular habitués who formed the Committee of Taste were famous, although the quality of the food was not always reliable since guests were used as guinea pigs for the doctor's culinary – and economical – experiments. To quote Jerdan: "A tureen of soup indeed, was not liked the better for having its ingredients explained and the price, perhaps 6d. or 7d. recorded (though, after all, it was fairly palatable and nutritious); but at any rate, it might be followed by a costly cut of Severn salmon, and there was generally a joint, to save you from experimenting on the made dishes, which I must own seemed often to be of dubious quality and rather dangerous to depend on for a man of appetite . . ."

Kitchiner's father had started life as a coal porter, but he quickly moved up the ladder, acquiring a tidy fortune as a coal merchant, and a social position – he became a Justice of the Peace. William, born in 1775, was the only son of his second marriage. He claimed to have been educated at Eton and Glasgow University where he was supposed to have studied medicine, but neither establishment has any record of his attendance. However, a comfortable income saved him the necessity of

OPPOSITE: BEEF A LA MODE AND POTATOES WITH ONIONS

earning his living and allowed him to devote himself to his hobbies. He married in 1799 but the union was not happy and the couple soon separated. He had an illegitimate son who was educated at Cambridge and who eventually inherited his property. The doctor was a prolific writer on all his chosen themes although the *Cook's Oracle* is the only one of his works to be still read. To quote the *Gentleman's Magazine* again:

"This amiable and useful man possessed the estimable virtue of never speaking ill of anyone – on the contrary, he was a lover of conciliation and to many proved a valuable advisor and firm friend. In manners he was quiet and apparently timid. As we have said however, he had three grand hobbies – cookery, music and optics – and whenever he entered upon either of them he was full, cheerful and even eloquent."

Judging by the opening paragraph of the introduction to the *Cook's Oracle* he certainly does not strike one as being timid:

"The following Receipts are not a mere marrowless collection of shreds and patches, and cuttings and pastings – but a bona fide register of Practical Facts – accumulated by a perseverance not to be subdued or evaporated by the igniferous terrors of a Roasting Fire in the Dog Days – in defiance of the odiferous and calefacient repellants of Roasting, – Boiling, – Frying, – and Broiling; – moreover the author has submitted to a labour no preceding Cookery Book maker, perhaps ever, attempted to encounter, – having *eaten* each Receipt before he set it down in his book." That no other cook book writer should have tested their recipes may seem a surprising claim, but it is substantially true of the late 18th and early 19th centuries when "receipts" were copied from book to book with little regard for accuracy and none for attribution. The doctor, however, intended to be more conscientious. His main thesis is that ill health arises not from the quality of the food that is eaten but from lack of care in its preparation:

"Among the multitude of causes which concur to impair Health, and produce Diseases, the most general is the improper quality of our Food; this most frequently arises from the injudicious manner in which it is prepared."

He then continues:

"The STOMACH is the mainspring of our System, – if it be not sufficiently wound up to warm the Heart and support the Circulation, – the whole business of Life will, in proportion be ineffectively performed, – we can neither *Think* with precision, – *Walk* with vigour, – *Sit Down* with comfort, – or *Sleep* with tranquillity. Unless *the Stomach* be in good humour, every part of the machinery of *Life* must vibrate with languor; – can we then be too attentive to its adjustment!!!"

His recommendations consist of a lengthy chapter of "friendly advice" to cooks that includes instructions on cleanliness, rigid time-keeping, respect for the employer, economy, menu planning, marketing and planning of the cooking. This is followed by a short chapter on weights and measures as the doctor insists that accurate measurements are essential for good cooking. There are then further chapters on boiling, baking, roasting (which he regards as the finest, and the most difficult, art of cookery), frying, vegetable cookery, fish, broths and soups, gravies and sauces and "made" dishes before we get to the bulk of the book, with its *tested* recipes.

Most of the doctor's recipes are in fact quite simple, depending for their flavor, which is usually excellent, on long slow cooking. This was easily and cheaply achieved in the corner of a range; in a modern kitchen a slow cookpot would serve admirably.

MOCK TURTLE SOUP
Serves 8

Real turtle soup was to Victorians rather what caviar is to us: a luxury to dream of rather than to taste. Indeed, as the *Encyclopedia Britannica* pointed out: "Turtles often become emaciated and sickly before they reach this country in which case the Soup would be incomparably improved by leaving out the turtle and substituting a good calf's head." Dr. Kitchiner gives several recipes for mock turtle soup, one of which "endeavored to imitate the excellent and generally approved Mock Turtle made by Messrs. Birch, Cornhill." However, since this took eight hours to make (one to clean and soak the calf's head; one to parboil it and cut it up; one to cool it; and five for making the broth and finishing the soup), I am suggesting his alternative recipe "as made by Elizabeth Lister (late Cook to Dr. Kitchiner), Bread and Biscuit Baker, No 6, Salcombe Place, York Terrace, Regent's Park. – Goes out to Dress Dinners on reasonable terms."

INGREDIENTS

2 lean slices of bacon
½ lb chuck beef, trimmed and cut up
*   roughly*
1 carrot, roughly chopped
1 sprig each of fresh lemon thyme,
*   winter savory and basil, or ½*
*   teaspoon of each dried, in a herb*
*   diffuser or tied in a piece of*
*   cheesecloth*
3 large sprigs of fresh parsley
15 allspice berries
15 black peppercorns
2 shallots, roughly chopped
1 large onion, stuck with 4 cloves
2 tablespoons all-purpose flour
½ cup medium sherry
juice of ½–1 lemon
about 2 teaspoons mushroom catsup
pinch of nutmeg
salt and black pepper

Put the bacon, beef, carrot, herbs, spices, shallots and onion in a large pan with ⅔ cup water. Bring to a boil and cook gently for 15 minutes. Add a further 2 quarts water, bring to a boil and simmer very gently for 2 hours.

In a bowl mix a little of the soup into the flour to make a paste, return this to the pan, blend thoroughly and cook for a further 30 minutes. Pass the soup through a fine strainer and return to a clean pan. You can pick the beef from the debris and return it to the soup if you wish. Add the sherry, then the lemon juice, mushroom catsup, and nutmeg, with salt and pepper to taste. Reheat gently and serve.

MACARONI PUDDING
Serves 8 as a starter, 4 as a main course

"One of the most elegant preparations of Macaroni is the *Timballe de Maccaroni*. This, we have been informed, is considered by a *Grand Gourmand,* as the most important recipe which was added to the collection of his Cook during a gastronomic tour through Europe: it is not an uncommon mode of preparing Maccaroni on the continent." Dr. Kitchiner serves his macaroni pudding accompanied by a brown sauce, which you may or may not feel improves it.

INGREDIENTS

2 cups macaroni
2 egg yolks plus 2 whole eggs
1¼ cups heavy cream
1 cup diced cooked chicken
¾ cup diced cooked ham
¾ cup grated fresh Parmesan
salt and pepper
handful of brown bread crumbs, well
*   toasted*

Cook the macaroni in plenty of fast boiling water until it is, as the doctor says, "tender; but take care not to have it too soft; though tender it should be firm, the form entirely preserved and no part beginning to melt." Drain it, but not too thoroughly.

Meanwhile, beat the egg yolks and whole eggs in a bowl with the cream. Add the chicken, ham and cheese, and season to taste with salt and pepper. Mix in the macaroni and turn the whole into a heatproof pie dish. Dr. Kitchiner then covers the pudding and steams it for 1 hour before serving; if you want a speedier method of cooking, cover it and microwave it on high for 5 to 6 minutes. Sprinkle the pudding with the bread crumbs and serve immediately.

WATER SOUCHY

Serves 8

A very popular Victorian cross between a soup and a stew. Dr. Kitchiner says that you should be able to "dress this dish of fish while the cloth is laying – twelve minutes will do it." This is true provided that you have already made your stock.

INGREDIENTS

8 whiting, boned and filleted but not
*   skinned*
2 quarts water
2 cups dry white wine
1 tablespoon anchovy paste
juice of 1½ lemons
2 medium onions, very finely chopped
3 bay leaves
3 sprigs of parsley plus a large handful,
*   finely chopped*
8 slices of whole-wheat bread, crusts
*   removed, toasted and cut in triangles*

Chop half the fish roughly and put it into a large pan with the water, wine, anchovy paste and lemon juice. Bring to a boil and simmer for 15 minutes. Strain and discard the fish. Cut the remaining fish into largish pieces and put them into a clean pan with the onions, bay leaf, sprigs of parsley and the strained stock from the first lot of fish. Bring to a boil slowly and simmer for 10 minutes. Remove the parsley sprigs and bay leaf before serving, sprinkled with the chopped parsley and accompanied by the "sippets" of toast.

ROAST PHEASANT WITH RICE SAUCE AND GRAVY

Serves 8

Dr. Kitchiner does not approve of pheasant: "... the character given it by an ingenious French author, is just as good as it deserves. 'Its flesh is naturally tough, and owes all its tenderness and succulence to the long time it is kept, before it is cooked; until it is *bien mortifié.*' It is uneatable." Maybe intensive breeding has done something for the pheasant, because in the 20th century it is regarded as somewhat of a delicacy. Both the gravy and the sauce can be made in advance.

INGREDIENTS

2 large cock or hen pheasants
butter or olive oil

Rub the breasts of the pheasants with a little butter or oil, cover them lightly with foil and roast them at 350° for 45 minutes. After 30 minutes, remove the foil so that the breasts can brown.

PHEASANT GRAVY

INGREDIENTS

1 slice of bacon, chopped
1 tablespoon butter
1 medium onion, roughly chopped
½ lb chuck beef, beaten with a mallet
*   and cut into large pieces*
3¾ cups boiling water
1 crust or slice of brown bread, toasted
1 sprig of parsley
1 sprig of thyme
rind of ½ lemon, pared with a
*   vegetable peeler*
6 allspice berries
6 black peppercorns
salt

Put the bacon into a heavy pan with the butter, onion and beef and cook briskly for 10 to 15 minutes until they are browned but not burned. Add the boiling water, toast, herbs, lemon rind, berries and peppercorns. Bring to a boil and simmer for 2 hours. Strain the sauce and adjust the seasoning with salt to taste before serving.

WATER SOUCHY (TOP LEFT) AND ROAST
PHEASANT WITH RICE SAUCE AND GRAVY

RICE SAUCE

INGREDIENTS

½ cup white rice
3¾ cups milk
1 medium onion
6 peppercorns
salt and white pepper
about ⅔ cup extra milk or water

Put the rice into a pan with the milk, onion and peppercorns. Bring to a boil and simmer until the rice is quite soft and all the liquid is absorbed. Remove the peppercorns, then blend in a food processor. To smooth the texture, rub the sauce through a strainer, then return to a clean pan. Season to taste with salt and pepper and thin the sauce a little with the extra milk or water. Reheat to serve with the pheasant.

A LA MODE BEEF OR VEAL
Serves 8

"In the 180 volumes on Cookery we patiently pioneered through, before we encountered the tremendous labour and expense of proving the receipts of our predecessors, we could not find one Receipt which approximated to anything like an accurate description of the way in which this excellent dish is actually dressed in the best A la Mode Beef Shops. However," writes the doctor, "after all, the whole of the secret seems to be thickening the gravy of Beef that has been very *slowly* stewed, and flavouring it with Bay leaves and Allspice."

INGREDIENTS

4½ lb chuck end of rib roast or breast of veal, boned, trimmed and cut into large pieces (about ¼ lb each)
about 6 heaped tablespoons seasoned flour
⅔ cup beef drippings or lard
4 large onions, finely minced
6¼ cups boiling water
4 large bay leaves, lightly crushed
12 allspice berries, lightly crushed

Toss the meat in the seasoned flour, making sure it is well covered. Melt the drippings or lard in a heavy pan, then add the onions and the meat and fry all briskly for about 8 minutes, or until the meat is well browned all over. Add a further 4 tablespoons of the flour and continue to cook for a few minutes, then add the boiling water. Stir well and make sure you incorporate all the bits sticking to the base of the pan. Add the bay leaves and allspice berries. Cover the pan, reduce the heat to very low and cook at just below a simmer for 3 to 3½ hours. Alternatively, transfer everything to a slow cooker for 6 to 8 hours. Allow the dish to cool completely and remove any excess fat.

To serve, reheat the beef, adjust the seasoning to taste and put it "in a tureen and it is ready for the table." The doctor suggests that it is accompanied by a "nice green salad."

RAISED HAM PIE
Serves 8

"This is, I think, a good way of dressing a small Ham, and has a good effect for a cold supper." Take heart, it is not nearly as much of a palaver as it appears and will look very impressive on a buffet table or as a "side dish" for your main meal.

INGREDIENTS

2¼ lb piece of lean ham, soaked in cold water for at least 2 hours, preferably longer
1¼ cups Marsala or medium sherry
about 2½ cups chicken or veal stock
1 cup very finely ground, well trimmed veal
⅓ cup beef or vegetable ground suet
⅔ cup water
1 tablespoon butter
½ cup whole-wheat flour
2 eggs, beaten
salt and pepper
pinch of nutmeg
1 tablespoon soft butter and 2 tablespoons flour worked into a paste
cayenne

PIE CRUST

2 cups whole-wheat flour
¼ cup butter
¼ cup lard
2 eggs

Drain the soaked ham, put it into a pan and cover generously with fresh cold water. Bring it to a boil and simmer for 30 minutes. Remove the ham, cool slightly, then remove the rind and any excess fat; discard the water. Return the ham to the pan with the Marsala or sherry and the stock. Bring to a boil and simmer gently for 2 hours. Remove from the heat and cool the ham in its cooking juices.

Meanwhile, mix the veal with the suet. Put the water in a pan with the butter, bring to a boil, then add the flour. Stir over a gentle heat until it forms a smooth but fairly solid paste. Add this mixture to the veal with the eggs, salt, pepper and nutmeg and mix very thoroughly, ideally in a food processor, to amalgamate the forcemeat.

To make the pie crust, rub the butter and lard into the flour, then bind the mixture with one of

the eggs, adding a little extra cold water if necessary. Roll out into a large enough piece to cover the ham and leave sufficient pastry to wrap it completely.

Use about one third of the veal forcemeat to make a bed the size of the ham on the pastry. Lift the ham out of its cooking juices and lay on the forcemeat. Reserve the juice. Use the remaining forcemeat to cover the top and the sides of the ham. Bring the pastry up the sides and over the top to make a parcel, trimming off any extra pieces of paste and securing the "joints" with a little cold water. Use the trimmings to garnish the pie and disguise any unseemly "joints." Beat the remaining egg lightly and use to paint the pastry very thoroughly. Lift carefully on to a baking sheet and bake at 325° for 1 hour; remove from the oven and leave the pie to become quite cool before serving.

Remove any fat from the top of the reserved cooking juices, then put into a pan with the butter and flour paste and cook till the sauce thickens. Season lightly with cayenne and add a little extra water to the sauce if it is too strong. Allow to cool and serve with the cold ham.

POTATOES

"The Vegetable Kingdom affords no Food more wholesome, more easily procured, easily prepared or less expensive than the Potato; yet although this most useful vegetable is dressed almost every day, in almost every family, – for One plate of Potatoes that comes to table as it should, Ten are spoiled." To remedy this state of affairs the doctor provides a wealth of advice on how to boil potatoes and then recipes for "sixteen ways of dressing them." Since he obviously felt so strongly on the subject I have chosen to include two of them.

POTATOES WITH ONIONS
Serves 8

INGREDIENTS

1 lb potatoes, boiled in their skins, then
    peeled and mashed, ideally through
    a ricer
2 cups finely minced onions – a food
    processor is ideal
¼ cup butter
salt and pepper

While the potatoes are cooking, put the onions into a pan with the butter and cook them very gently until they are quite soft – this should take about 15 minutes. Beat the cooked onions into the mashed potatoes and season to taste. Reheat before serving.

POTATO BALLS RAGOUT
Serves 8

"An agreeable vegetable relish, and a good supper dish."

INGREDIENTS

2 tablespoons butter
¾ cup very finely diced cooked ham
1 large onion, minced
2 egg yolks
1 lb potatoes, boiled in their skins, then
    peeled and mashed, ideally through
    a ricer
salt and pepper
pinch of nutmeg
about 4 tablespoons fresh brown bread
    crumbs
clarified butter or oil to fry

Beat the butter, ham, onion and egg yolks into the potato and season to taste. Roll the mixture into walnut-sized balls and coat in the bread crumbs. Heat a little butter or oil in a shallow pan and gently fry the potato balls until they are well browned on all sides. Serve immediately or reheat gently in a moderate oven before serving.

RICE BLANCMANGE

Serves 6 to 8

Dr. Kitchiner does not approve of desserts as they "waste a great deal of a cook's time and achieve little in the way of nourishment." Consequently there is a very meager sprinkling of dessert recipes at the end of the book, mostly of the nourishing "nursery" pudding class. Even among these the rice blancmange is the only one to receive any commendation at all:

"This dish is much approved of; it is eaten with cream or custard, and preserved fruits – raspberries are best. It should be made the day before it is wanted, that it may get firm."

INGREDIENTS

¾ cup short-grain white rice
3¾ cups whole milk
2 tablespoons extra-fine sugar
rind of 1 lemon, thinly pared
¼ teaspoon cinnamon
2½ cups heavy cream
3 cups preserved raspberries, cherries,
*   currants, strawberries or any other*
*   well-flavored soft fruit*

Note If you cannot get interesting preserved fruit, use canned raspberries or black cherries with 3–4 tablespoons of brandy added to the syrup.

Put the rice in a bowl with just enough water to cover and leave to soak for 30 minutes. Turn it into a heavy pan, add the milk, sugar, lemon rind and cinnamon and cook very gently for 30 to 40 minutes, or until all the liquid is absorbed and the rice is very soft. If necessary add a little more milk or water.

Rinse out a fancy mold with cold water and spoon the rice into it. It should turn out fairly easily but if you are nervous, line the mold with plastic wrap. Cool and chill in the refrigerator. Unmold the blancmange on to a decorative serving plate, and serve accompanied by lots of cream and the fruit.

————————

OPPOSITE: COLLEGE PUDDINGS WITH
WINE SAUCE AND RICE BLANCMANGE WITH
CREAM

————————

COLLEGE PUDDINGS

Serves 8

These batter puddings are rather like sweet Yorkshire puddings, and although they will heat up reasonably satisfactorily, they are much better if served straight from the oven.

INGREDIENTS

4 medium eggs
½ cup all-purpose flour
3 tablespoons extra-fine sugar
pinch of nutmeg
pinch of ginger
⅓ cup brandy
¼ cup milk
1 cup raisins, plumped if they are dry
⅔ cup ground suet

Preheat the oven to 375°. Whip the eggs in a bowl with the flour, sugar, nutmeg and ginger until you have a smooth batter. Add the brandy and milk, then the raisins and suet. Grease the insides of sixteen "patty pans" or muffin pans lightly and use a ladle to spoon in the mixture, making sure the raisins and suet are distributed evenly. Bake for 25 to 30 minutes, or until the puddings are puffed and browned. Serve immediately with a warm wine sauce (see below).

WINE SAUCE

INGREDIENTS

2 cups medium sweet white wine
10 tablespoons unsalted butter
2–3 tablespoons extra-fine sugar

Put the ingredients into a small saucepan and heat until the butter has melted. Simmer for 10 minutes to reduce slightly, then taste for sweetness. Serve with the College Puddings or any other steamed or baked dessert.

DINING ROOMS
AND THEIR FURNISHINGS

Not until the end of the 18th century did dining-rooms as such exist even in the greatest of English houses. As late as the 1790s, when meals were to be served, trestle or folding tables were set up in the middle of the room and benches, stools or chairs which were stored against the walls were drawn up around them. Admittedly, by the end of the century, the "suites" of dining furniture – sideboards, urns, chairs and so on – designed by the Adam brothers, Thomas Chippendale and Hepplewhite had become *de rigueur* in all the best houses, but it was not until Victoria ascended the throne that a dining room became a regular feature in every middle class house.

Indeed it was not until Victoria's reign that it became usual to place furniture informally around a room rather than lining it all up against the walls – a practice that would have been quite impracticable with the large heavy dining room tables we associate with the 19th century. These massive pieces of furniture, usually in walnut, mahogany or rosewood, with sturdy central pillars and ornate clawed feet, were mostly round with a center section that could be inserted to increase their size. Chairs were equally ornate with intricately carved (and uncomfortable) backs and legs and padded upholstered seats. A set would normally comprise two "carvers" with arms and anywhere from four to twenty ordinary chairs.

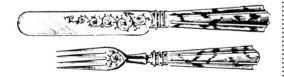

The sideboard completed the major furnishing of the dining room. The early Adam or Hepplewhite examples were capacious but relatively delicate. They included compartments for bottles and the storage of plate and linen, and often a lead-lined drawer to hold water in which to rinse glasses, but they had slender legs and gave an overall appearance of elegance. How-

ever, as the 19th century progressed, the legs disappeared into more cupboards and the sideboard acquired a heavy and often elaborately carved back piece. Doors and fronts grew more cumbersome too and acquired decorations of their own until the whole piece could take up a complete wall of a room.

Table settings, like the furniture, grew in elaboration with the century. The 1700s had seen the blossoming of English tableware with fine silver and the beautiful porcelain and pottery produced by the factories at Bow, Spode, Worcester, Chelsea, Derby, and of course, Josiah Wedgwood's establishment at Etruria. So successful had Wedgwood been in developing a relatively tough but delicate earthenware – his "cream" or "Queen's" ware – that by the 1830s there was no reason why even an only moderately well-to-do family could not own a complete set of attractive table crockery.

Cutlery had also been refined during the 18th century, when it became the accepted method of conveying the food to the mouth – even as recently as Queen Anne's day, many people used only a knife and their fingers. Three-pronged forks and knife blades were mainly made in steel, with elaborately carved and decorated ivory, bone and porcelain handles. Silver, pewter and the new alloy, Britannia metal, were used for spoons, ladles, slotted spatulas and serving implements. The development of a harder nickel-silver alloy in the mid 19th century provided an alternative to the efficient but labor-intensive steel for the blades and prongs of mass-produced knives and forks. However, right to the end of Victoria's reign, one of the daily and time-consuming tasks of the butler, footman or upstairs maid in any household was to clean the steel cutlery.

Silver and pewter had always been used for the serving dishes, and these, like the sideboards on which they stood, became increasingly ornate. Silver candlesticks, often with fringed silk shades on the candles, cruet sets, finger bowls, fruit baskets and so on appeared in greater or lesser profusion according to the wealth of the family. The 19th century also saw the development of the "epergne" or ornamental centerpiece for the table, incorporating branches and small dishes to hold nuts, fruits or sweetmeats. As with everything else in the dining room, the epergnes grew ever larger. Some of the later structures are so massive that they could scarcely be lifted from the table – and must certainly have inhibited any conversation across them!

Glassware, too, had come of age during the 18th century, when it supplanted silver and pewter for most drinking vessels, bottles and decanters. A tax on the weight of each glass, with the exception of those made by the Waterford glass factory in Ireland where it was not levied, ensured that all 18th and early 19th century glassware was light and delicate, employing colored glass, twists and bubbles for decoration. Fluted

THE DINNER TABLE, CAREFULLY LAID FOR A FAMILY MEAL IN 1888

and stemmed glasses (usually with short stems and bucket-shaped bowls) were used for wines, jellies and sweetmeats. In 1845 the glass tax was finally removed and cut glass became the rage. As a result, later Victorian glass was immensely heavy with deeply cut and incised decoration.

Since medieval times, dining tables had been covered with white cloths, and in this the Victorians followed the customs of their forefathers. Tablecloths reached to the floor and were laid over thick green baize undercloths to protect the table. Napkins were ample, starched and usually folded into intricate shapes to ornament the table further.

A DINNER AT THE REFORM CLUB WITH ALEXIS SOYER

"At present we do not know of any person," wrote a reporter in the *Observer* in 1848 when Soyer had just left the Reform Club, a famous Liberal club, "who administers more assiduously and effectively to our corporal wants – at least the most craving of them – than the renowned Soyer . . . Now that he has abandoned the service of the Reform Club we see him erecting soup kitchens for a famishing nation; inventing a 'magic stove' for the benefit of the affluent classes; distilling a cooling water to 'quench the spark in the throat,' and compounding a sauce that undoubtedly will prove a 'relish' to the most used-up of palates ... M. Soyer is an artist as profound as he is versatile."

A no less heartfelt, if slightly less mellifluous, testimony comes from William Thackeray through the pen of George Augustus Sala, the journalist:
"Thackeray had towards Soyer the friendliest feelings and genuine admiration to boot; since the mercurial Frenchman was something more than an excellent cook – that is to say, Alexis was a man of sound commonsense, a practical organiser, a racy humorist and a constant sayer of good things."

One can understand how such affection could be inspired by a great chef who, once his night's work at the Reform Club was complete, would change his clothes, rush off to the opera with his friends and be found hours later walking home, cracking jokes and eating bread and cheese or fried fish out of a newspaper packet.

OPPOSITE: GALANTINE DE POUSSIN A LA VOLIERE (LEFT) AND RIS D'AGNEAU PIQUE AUX POINTES D'ASPERGES ET AUX CONCOMBRES

Alexis Benoit Soyer was born in 1809 in a little town north-east of Paris, the youngest son of a small shopkeeper and destined, as soon as he proved himself to have a good singing voice, for the church – a career which did not appeal to the young Soyer. To escape he managed to get himself expelled from school (by ringing the local church bell – the fire alarm – at midnight) and headed for Paris where his brother, Philippe, was apprenticed as a chef.

For lack of anything immediately better, Alexis also became apprenticed and worked first at Chez Grignon for four years and then at Douix' restaurant on the Boulevard des Italiens for three years. He could not have had, to quote Messrs. Volant and Warren, his biographers, "a sounder training than at these noted houses where they have to go through the rough part of the business and are generally hard worked but where, ultimately, the intelligent and clever are sure to be promoted."

Promoted Alexis duly was – to the Foreign Office. But no sooner had he taken up his post than the 1830 revolution broke over him, necessitating a hasty retreat across the channel to England where his brother Philippe was already working. After a couple of temporary posts in London he became chef to a Mr. Lloyd of Aston Hall near Oswestry where he remained for four happy and successful years. However, Soyer was at heart a city man, and in 1835 he returned to London for a year's service with the gourmet Marquis of Ailsa at Isleworth before taking up a post which fulfilled his every dream – the chef at the Reform Club. This gave him the chance to plan and run the kitchens of the new and grandiose building (inspired by the Farnese Palace in Rome) being designed by Charles Barry.

Soyer was to remain at the Reform Club for nearly fifteen years, during which time his enduring reputation was made. The "matchless culinary arrangements" of the kitchens he designed inspired eulogies from hordes of aristocratic visitors whom he delighted in taking on conducted tours. One of them, the Vicomtesse de Malleville, wrote in the *Courrier de l'Europe:* "The kitchen is as spacious as a ballroom, kept in the finest order. Around you the water boils and stewpans bubble ... and a little farther on is a moveable furnace before which pieces of meat are transformed into savoury *rôtis*; in the distance Dutch ovens, marble mortars, lighted stoves, iced plates of metal for fish and various compartments for vegetables, fruits and spices ..." Certainly the detailed plans and explanations of each larder, cupboard, stove and preparation area that Soyer provides in the *Gastronomic Regenerator* evoke the profoundest admiration even today.

Early in his career at the Reform Club Soyer decided to marry. Having chanced upon no lady who took his fancy in England, he thought he should have his portrait painted and sent to an old flame in Paris. Recommended to a Flemish portrait painter in London, Soyer went for his first sitting and promptly fell passionately in love with the painter's stepdaughter, Emma Jones, a talented portrait painter in her own right. Despite some initial opposition from her stepfather, Emma and Alexis were married in 1837. The couple were well suited and blissfully happy, but the marriage was not to last. To Soyer's lasting desolation, Emma died in childbirth in August 1842.

After Emma's death Soyer moved in with her stepfather, the painter Simonau, with whom he was by then on the best of terms. He had always been flamboyant, eager to shock or surprise and, above all, to be different but now this desire became almost obsessional. He designed his clothes himself – his coats cut on the cross with ever deeper cuffs, his cravats "triumphs of ingenuity," his waistcoats gold-embroidered velvet or white satin worked with colored silks. His hats, cigar case, cane and visiting cards were all fashioned so that there should not be a single parallel line.

In 1845 Soyer produced his first slim volume of culinary essays, *Délassements Culinaires,* but this, he promised, was to be followed by something much more substantial. *The Gastronomic Regenerator* which appeared the following year was certainly more substantial – over two thousand recipes. It was written in an amazing ten months – the more amazing when one realizes that at the same time Soyer was running a large and busy kitchen. A team of three was responsible for its composition. Soyer's first kitchen maid, who had been with him for years, and his first apprentice prepared the dishes according to Soyer's receipts and wrote them down; Soyer then revised them, adding his own comments.

The book is divided into two parts: the "Kitchen of the Wealthy" (from which I have taken this menu) and a much shorter section on the "Kitchen at Home." Every aspect of cookery is dealt with in turn and in detail and Soyer also gives comprehensive plans and instructions for the design of the kitchen at the Reform Club, a kitchen "at home," a "bachelor's kitchen" and a "cottage kitchen." The book was a great success and was in its fourth edition by March 1847.

Meanwhile, Soyer's energy had found a new outlet in "inventing things." His designs for the Reform Club kitchen had included much that was new and ingenious; now his fertile imagination produced Cooking Clocks, Patent Egg Cooking machines, Magic Coffee Pots, Chimney Screw Jacks, Improved Baking Dishes, various stoves both for domestic and military use (his field kitchen which he designed in the Crimea was still in use during the Second World War), a cottager's stove capable of "baking, boiling, roasting, washing, ironing, drying linen and warming rooms of any size" and, most famous of all, his "magic stove." The *Morning Post* found this tiny spirit stove, still known in every restaurant as a chafing dish, "so certain and cleanly in its operations that a gentleman may cook his steak on the study table, or a lady may have it among her crochet or other work." Yet another enterprise were his sauces and relishes, the recipes for which Soyer sold for a few pounds to his friends, Mr. Crosse and Mr. Blackwell, who subsequently marketed them *most* successfully.

Then, in 1847, came the Irish potato famine. Soyer had already devoted some time to teaching "charitably inclined ladies" how to make nourishing soups for the poor. Early in 1837 he had originated a public subscription for a soup kitchen in Leicester Square (using his newly invented soup boiler) which was soon supplying forty to fifty gallons of soup daily to two to three hundred people. By June 1847 the Irish were dying in their thousands and the government invited Soyer to submit a plan for a new soup kitchen to be used for their relief. The Reform Club gave him leave of absence and the spring of 1848 saw Soyer successfully catering to over eight thousand people daily from his newly designed Dublin kitchens.

While in Ireland Soyer published *The Poor Man's Regenerator,* a little sixpenny booklet (the profits from which were all donated to charity) that included not only the recipes for his famous soups (and revolutionary instructions to use, not throw out, vegetable peelings in the process) but also for economical stews, puddings, breads and so on. The booklet was so successful that on his return to London Soyer was inundated with requests to establish similar projects in the poorer London parishes. Various schemes were launched but none received sufficient support to ever really get under way.

SOYER'S SAUCE,

~~sold only in the above bottles, holding half-a-pint.~~
PRICE 2s. 6d.

In 1849 his next book, *The Modern Housewife,* appeared. This was aimed at the middle class housewife. The book is designed as a correspondence between "Hortense" or "Mrs. B.," the perfect modern housewife, and her friend "Eloise" or "Mrs. L." Hortense offers advice, recipes and suggestions to her less competent friend. These become more elaborate as the "B's" position in the world improves. The book was in its second edition within a fortnight and continued to sell in large quantities for many years. With each new edition new recipes and ideas were added. In 1853 when the thirty thousandth "edition" was brought out, Soyer added a whole new section in which the "B's" fortunes had taken a sad turn for the worse – they were reduced to one servant and a small cottage outside Rugby – thus giving him a chance to revamp his *Poor Man's Regenerator* to fit the "B's" reduced circumstances.

In 1850 Soyer, to the consternation of the press and public, left the Reform Club because of a disagreement as to whether the public should be allowed into the coffee rooms. His reputation was at its zenith and once freed from the restraints of the Club, his services were in constant demand to organize grandiose banquets all over the country. Wise friends suggested that he "take a house and give therein, without any claptrap show or external demonstration, *the best dinners* that a man could get in London – you will make your fortune." But that was too tame for Soyer who first planned a "College of Domestic Economy," which had to be abandoned for lack of capital, and then became involved in a far more costly enterprise: "The Gastronomic Symposium of all Nations."

This venture was inspired by the Great Exhibition of 1851. Soyer had originally tendered for the official contract to feed the visitors to the Great Exhibition but when he discovered how restricted his facilities would be, he changed his mind. Instead he took the lease of Gore House, a few hundred yards from the exhibition site, and proceeded to spend a fortune on transforming (if not always in the best taste) an already magnificent house. The Symposium duly opened in May and bemused visitors gawped at the Transatlantic Antechamber "supplying every kind of American beverage;" the Grotte des Neiges Eternelles where "craggy masses of stalactites hung glistening with the crystallized brilliance of ice;" the Boudoir de la Vallière with a "fluted white and blue satin ceiling heightened with silver, and walls that presented a curious yet beautiful pattern of zigzag stripes and broad diagonal bands of black and silver lace" and the Baronial Banqueting Hall, "100 foot long, 50 foot wide and 30 foot high, whose roof was entirely of stained glass and whose walls were covered with rich crimson drapery . . ."

The Symposium was, understandably, as much of an attraction as the Exhibition and was constantly crowded with up to five hundred members of the public, as well as private groups for whom Soyer would arrange special dinners. However, the Symposium had cost a fortune and its future after the exhibition closed had to be in doubt. The death blow was delivered by Mr. Pownall, the Chairman of the Middlesex Sessions, who arrived on a particularly busy and rowdy night to decide whether the license for the Symposium, which had only been obtained with the greatest difficulty, should be renewed. Alas, its charms were wasted on Mr. Pownall, who declared that he "had never been witness to such disgraceful dissipation in my life." Soyer was distraught and furious and in a typical gesture closed the doors of the Symposium on October 14 never to reopen them. The bills were enormous but, strictly honorable, Soyer settled them all from his own pocket, leaving himself, as he told a friend, with barely £100. Gore House was bought by the Great Exhibition Committee with the profits made from the exhibition, and on its site the Albert Hall now stands.

After the closure of the Symposium, Soyer once again took to organizing banquets and dinners throughout the country and to compiling yet another book, although there is now some doubt as to how much of this work was his own. *The Pantropheon, or the History of Food and its Preparation from the Earliest Ages of the World* was a "vast compendium of scraps and learned references dealing with every kind of aliment from the dawn of time." It was well received but, understandably, not as popular as his next publication, *Soyer's Shilling Cookery,* which came out in 1854 and which had sold an unbelievable quarter of a million copies by 1867. The book was written for "the artisan, mechanic and cottager" and its recipes are admirably simple, lucid, cheap and yet varied.

In May 1854 the Crimean War had got under

way and by the end of the year horrendous tales were filtering back to England of the conditions suffered by the troops. In January 1855 a letter appeared in *The Times* from a soldier at the front asking Soyer's help in cooking their rations. Soyer's interest was aroused and he started to read the dispatches from the front, with increasing horror. In February he offered his services to the government, free of charge, to see what he could do to improve the situation. His offer was accepted.

Soyer arrived at Scutari in the spring of 1855 and spent two years in the Crimea revolutionizing a system of provisioning that obliged orderlies to tie "scissors, half a dozen buttons, forks or a pair of old candle snuffers" to their rations of meat before they went into the boiler so that they could recognize them when they came out, and that threw out the fat which was left on the top of the boilers after cooking, deeming it "useless." Soyer's designs for new kitchens, his inventions, difficulties and escapades are all chronicled in the last of his books, *Culinary Campaigns,* which he wrote on his return to England – and which makes highly entertaining reading. But during those two years he also earned the love and respect of thousands of soldiers whose rations he transformed from inedible greasy lumps of tough meat and watery gruel into warm and nourishing soups and stews, puddings and broths; of the government who had sent him out there; and of Florence Nightingale. On his death three years later she wrote:

"His death is a great disaster. Others have studied cooking for the purpose of gormandising, some for show but none but he for the purpose of cooking large quantities of food in the most nutritious manner for great numbers of men. He has no successor."

The Crimea was Soyer's last fling. While there he caught Crimean fever from which he never really recovered, although he insisted on returning to work in his kitchens. He came back to England in 1857 where he was much fêted and where he continued to invent, advise and cook, as well as finishing the *Culinary Campaign.* But he was not well and a riding accident in the late summer of that year hastened a decline that resulted in his death in August 1858.

"Kindly, erratic, frivolous, warm-hearted Alexis Soyer," George Augustus Sala wrote after his funeral. "He quacked, certainly, – puffed himself and his eccentricity in all kinds of ways – but he never derogated one iota from his dignity as an honest man. He was no vulgar charlatan for he was full of inventive ingenuity . . . He didn't do any one any harm. He did, on the contrary, a vast amount of good in his generation: and even those who laughed at him loved him for his simple childlike ways and generous candour. He was an original."

BILL OF FARE

Soyer makes a point in the *Gastronomic Regenerator* of only giving three bills of fare (the majority of contemporary cookery books included dozens): a dinner from his "Table at Home," a "Lucullusian dinner" which is far beyond our highest aspirations, and a dinner to "grace the Table of the Wealthy" – and to show off his "pagodatique service." This service or dish was one of Soyer's favorite inventions. It consisted of an oriental-shaped, covered dish with a largish central bowl and four smaller side bowls. The purpose was to put the entrée in the center with the appropriate sauces around it. Heat-retaining silver sand was stored in the base of the dish so that the pagodatique dish, if placed in a heated cupboard for a couple of hours, could then keep food hot for up to an hour. The entrées are designed to be served in such a dish, some with four sauces, some with two that would "double up" in the sauce dishes.

POTAGE A LA VICTORIA
Serves 8 to 10

INGREDIENTS

2 tablespoons butter
about 1¾ lb meaty beef or veal bones,
  well broken up
about 1 lb neck of lamb, roughly
  chopped
⅔ cup roughly chopped bacon or ham
1 medium onion, roughly chopped
1 small turnip, roughly chopped
1 carrot, roughly chopped
2 celery stalks, roughly chopped
1 bay leaf
handful of parsley sprigs
½ teaspoon salt
2½ quarts water
1 small cooking or large tart eating
  apple, chopped but not peeled
3 artichoke hearts
2 large anchovies
½ cup pearl barley
1 heaped tablespoon arrowroot
2 handfuls of parsley, finely chopped
1 teaspoon extra-fine sugar
½ cup heavy cream
salt and pepper

Melt the butter in a large pan and briskly fry the bones, lamb, bacon or ham and vegetables for a few minutes until they are all lightly browned. Add the bay leaf, parsley and salt, then pour in the water slowly. Bring to a boil and simmer for 1 hour. Add the apple, artichoke hearts and anchovies and simmer for a further hour, then strain through a fine strainer. You can freeze the strained stock.

To finish the soup, add the pearl barley to the stock, bring to a boil and simmer for 30 minutes. Mix the arrowroot with a little of the soup in a small bowl and add to the pan. Cook for a further 15 minutes. Add the parsley, sugar and cream and season to taste.

TURBOT EN MATELOTE VIERGE

Serves 8 as part of the complete menu, 4 as a main course

The sauce provides a very rich but very delicious "white overcoat" for the turbot, and if you have the energy to prepare all the garnishes, this is really a dish fit for a king. You could substitute halibut or sole for the turbot. The sauce can be prepared in advance and even frozen provided the finishing touches are left until just before it is served.

INGREDIENTS

1 small sole or two largish fillets of sole
⅓ cup dry white wine
slice of lemon
1 onion, very finely chopped
¾ cup medium sherry
1 clove
2 blades of mace
1 sprig of parsley
1 bay leaf
pinch of nutmeg
1½ tablespoons butter
2⅓ tablespoons all-purpose flour
2½ cups milk
pinch of salt
pinch of sugar
juice of ½ lemon
⅔ cup heavy cream
4 turbot steaks

GARNISH

¼ lb whitebait (optional)
seasoned flour
oil for frying
8 oysters or mussels (optional)
beaten egg
fresh brown bread crumbs
2 tablespoons butter

To make the sauce, fillet the sole if you are using a whole one. Ideally, put the bones and skin in a pan with some water, the white wine and slice of lemon and boil briskly for 10 minutes to make some stock. Alternatively, you can use the wine mixed with water. Put the fillets of fish in a heavy pan with the onion, sherry, clove, mace, parsley, bay leaf and nutmeg. Bring to a boil and cook at a fast boil for 5 minutes.

Meanwhile, make some béchamel sauce by melting the butter in another pan, adding the flour and cooking for a few minutes, before adding the milk gradually. Continue to cook and stir until the sauce thickens. Add the béchamel sauce to the fish mixture and simmer for 20 minutes, stirring occasionally. Rub the mixture through a strainer, then add 1¼ cups of the fish stock. Simmer for a further 30 minutes, or until the sauce thickens slightly – do not worry if it appears to curdle. Season with salt, pepper and the lemon juice. At this point you can set the sauce aside for future use. To finish the sauce, re-heat it gently, stirring continuously. Whip the cream until it just holds its shape and stir into the sauce. Adjust the seasoning if necessary.

Dry the whitebait carefully on paper towels, then toss in some well-seasoned flour. Deep fry in clean oil until they are crisp and browned, then drain on more paper towels. They can be kept warm in a cool oven for up to an hour quite successfully. Alternatively, they can be cooked 2 hours in advance and reheated successfully in a hot oven for 10 to 15 minutes.

Dry the oysters or mussels on paper towels. Coat liberally in beaten egg, then roll in plenty of fresh brown bread crumbs. Melt 2 tablespoons butter in a heavy pan and fry the shellfish on both sides gently until they are firm and browned. They will keep for up to 30 minutes in a warm oven.

Soyer tells one to boil the turbot but I find steaming a better method. Steam the steaks over a mixture of water and white wine with a slice of lemon for 7 to 10 minutes, depending on the thickness of the steaks. Bone them carefully and serve them with the sauce spooned over and garnished with the whitebait and oysters or mussels.

RIS D'AGNEAU PIQUE AUX POINTES D'ASPERGES ET AUX CONCOMBRES

Serves 8

Soyer uses lamb sweetbreads but if you wanted to make the dish even more delicious – and expensive – you could use calf. The sauces can be made in advance and reheated; the sweetbreads should be cooked just before they are served.

INGREDIENTS

1 tablespoon olive oil
4 slices of bacon
2 medium onions, finely chopped
handful of parsley, chopped
½ teaspoon dried thyme
2 bay leaves
salt and pepper
2 lb lamb or calf sweetbreads, cleaned and sliced if you are using calf
1¼ cups good chicken or veal stock or white wine and water mixed

Spread the oil over the bottom of a wide shallow pan, then cover with the bacon rashers. Mix the onions, parsley, thyme and bay leaves together and spread over the bacon. Season well. Lay the sweetbreads on top and pour over the stock or wine and water. Bring to a boil and simmer gently for 15 minutes. Remove the sweetbreads with a perforated spoon and serve accompanied by the following sauces.

CUCUMBER SAUCE

INGREDIENTS

1 medium cucumber, peeled and seeds removed
2 tablespoons butter
½ teaspoon extra-fine sugar
3 shallots, chopped
about 1¼ cups veal or chicken stock or white wine and water mixed
1¼ cups béchamel sauce (page 145)
⅓ cup heavy cream
salt and pepper

Cut the cucumber into small matchsticks. Melt the butter and sugar in a pan and add the shallots and cucumber; cook gently without allowing either vegetable to color for 10 minutes. Add enough stock or wine and water to cover the cucumber, cover the pan and simmer for about 15 minutes, or until the cucumber is tender. Drain the cucumber mixture and reserve the cooking liquid. Return ⅔ cup of this to the pan and add the béchamel. Bring to a boil and simmer for 10 minutes, or until the sauce is somewhat reduced. Add the cream and seasoning to taste, then add the cucumber and reheat before serving.

ASPARAGUS SAUCE

INGREDIENTS

12 oz can asparagus tips, drained
5 tablespoons butter
1 tablespoon all-purpose flour
1¼ cups béchamel sauce (page 145)
⅔ cup chicken or veal stock or water and white wine mixed
salt and white pepper
½ teaspoon sugar

Put the asparagus into a pan with 4 tablespoons of the butter and stir over a low heat until the asparagus is entirely mushed. Add the flour, mix well, then add the béchamel and the stock or water and wine. Bring to a boil and simmer for 5 minutes, then rub through a fine strainer. Return the sauce to a clean pan, season to taste with salt, pepper and the sugar and add the remaining butter just before reheating to serve. Reheat quickly or the sauce will lose its color.

LES CAILLES AUX FEUILLES DE VIGNES

Serves 8 as part of the complete menu, 4 as a main course

Soyer kept his quails moist by skewering them, then wrapping them in vine leaves and bacon and burying them in a parcel of chopped mixed vegetables before spit-roasting them. One can achieve the same excellent effect rather less laboriously by casserole-roasting them, sunk deep in a bed of chopped vegetables. He served his birds in a circle on a bed of stewed cabbage, surrounded by green beans, with a pyramid of green peas in the middle and accompanied by a white jardinière sauce that is so full of vegetables that it really qualifies as a vegetable in its own right. Since this menu is only about a third of Soyer's original one and white sauces are already used in several dishes, I have substituted a classic brown jardinière (see opposite) for the white one.

INGREDIENTS

8 quails, cleaned and trussed
8 large vine leaves
8 strips bacon
4 tablespoons olive oil
2 large onions, finely chopped
3 large carrots, finely chopped
2 turnips, finely chopped
3 celery stalks, finely chopped
6 mushrooms, finely chopped
large sprig of parsley, chopped
salt and pepper
1 lb lightly cooked green beans
    (optional)
1¼ cups lightly cooked green peas
    (optional)

Wrap each bird first in a vine leaf and then in a strip of bacon. Heat the oil in a heavy flameproof casserole just large enough to hold the quail and cook the vegetables briskly for about 5 minutes until they are just starting to color, then season them lightly. Bury the quail in the vegetables, taking care to leave a thin layer under each bird, and roast them, uncovered, at 375° for 35 minutes. Soyer does not specifically instruct one to remove the bacon and vine leaves so you can serve the quail with or without their "coats."

If you wish to reproduce the dish in all its glory, arrange the quails in a circle on the bed of cabbage (see below) surrounded by the beans and with a pyramid of peas in the middle. Alternatively, arrange the birds on the cabbage and use some of the vegetables with which they were cooked as garnish.

STEWED CABBAGE

INGREDIENTS

1 tablespoon butter
1 large onion, finely chopped
1 large carrot, very finely diced
5 strips of bacon, very finely chopped
handful of parsley, finely chopped
1 teaspoon dried thyme
1 bay leaf
5 whole cloves
3½ cups fairly finely chopped green
    cabbage
salt and pepper
⅔ cup chicken or veal stock or white
    wine and water mixed

Melt the butter in a heavy pan and gently cook the onion, carrot, bacon, herbs and cloves for about 15 minutes – they should be slightly softened but not burned. Add the cabbage, season it well and then add the stock. Mix the cabbage and stock thoroughly with the other vegetables, cover the pan and simmer for 45 minutes. Remove the lid and cook for a further 5 to 10 minutes to reduce any excess stock before serving.

JARDINIERE SAUCE

INGREDIENTS

*4 medium carrots, diced small
1 teaspoon sugar
4 tablespoons butter
3 turnips, diced small
15–20 pearl onions
2 cups good beef consommé (you can
   use good quality canned)
1¼ cups good brown sauce (page 145)
2 tablespoons green peas
handful of green beans, lightly cooked
8 small flowerets of cauliflower, lightly
   cooked
8 asparagus tips (optional)
salt and pepper*

LES CAILLES AUX FEUILLES DE VIGNES WITH STEWED CABBAGE AND JARDINIERE SAUCE

Boil the carrots briskly for 10 minutes, then drain. Melt the sugar and butter in a pan and add the carrots, turnips and onions. Cover them and cook gently for 20 minutes. Add 1¼ cups of the consommé and simmer until the vegetables are tender – about 30 minutes. Strain the vegetables and set them aside. Return the cooking juices to the pan and add the brown sauce and the remaining consommé. Bring to a boil and boil briskly for 15 minutes to reduce the sauce until it is fairly thick. Return the vegetables to the pan with the peas, beans, cauliflower and asparagus. Simmer for a further 10 minutes and adjust the seasoning to taste before serving.

FILET DE CANETON, SAUCE AU JUS D'ORANGE

Serves 8 as part of the complete menu, 4 as a main course

Soyer's recipe calls for wild ducks but farmed birds will do very well although they will be richer. As usual the recipe assumes that you will have sauces on hand but if you are also following M. Soyer's other recipes, you will need them anyhow. Surprisingly, the sauce is very light and a good foil to the richness of the duck.

INGREDIENTS

> 4 wild ducks or 2 farmed ducks
> mixture of finely chopped vegetables
>   such as onion, carrot, parsnip, turnip,
>   mushroom and tomato (enough to
>   form thick bed for ducks)
> 1 cup medium sherry
> large bunch of parsley
> 5 cups consommé (good quality canned
>   will do)
> 2½ cups good brown sauce (page 145)
> pinch of sugar
> rind of 2 oranges, cut into very fine
>   strips and blanched in boiling water
>   for 2 minutes
> about 1 tablespoon orange juice
> salt and pepper

Prick the ducks all over and lay them, on the bed of vegetables, on a rack over a baking pan; roast them at 375°, allowing 18 minutes per pound. Then remove the breast fillets and set them aside to be carved. Remove all the leg and back meat, chop it finely and put into a large pan with the sherry and parsley. Bring to the boil and simmer for 5 minutes. Add the consommé, boil the mixture for 10 minutes, skim if necessary, then simmer for a further 30 minutes. The sauce should then have reduced considerably. Add the brown sauce with a pinch of sugar and the orange rind and juice. Cook for a further few minutes, then season to taste. To serve, slice the duck breasts neatly and warm the slices very carefully in a covered dish – 2 minutes in a microwave would be ideal – and spoon over the sauce.

GALANTINE DE POUSSIN A LA VOLIERE

Serves 8 as part of the complete menu, 4 as a main course

The recipe in the *Gastronomic Regenerator* is actually for a turkey but since the menu specifies poussin, I have reduced the quantities accordingly; you could of course double or treble them for a larger bird. Soyer uses a veal forcemeat as stuffing. If you do not have the time or energy to make this, substitute well seasoned and very well trimmed ground veal or good quality sausage-meat.

INGREDIENTS

> 1 large poussin or very small (2¼ lb)
>   chicken, completely boned out with
>   its legs and wing meat pushed back
>   into the body of the bird and the
>   apertures sewn up
> about 1 lb forcemeat (see opposite),
>   ground veal or good sausage meat
> about ¼ cup lean cooked ham, cut in
>   strips
> 4 slices of fatty bacon, cut in strips
> about 20 pistachio nuts
> 3 tablespoons truffles (if you can afford
>   them!) or black mushrooms, cut in
>   strips
> salt and pepper
> about 5 cups good veal or chicken stock
>   (optional)
> 2 onions
> 2 carrots
> bouquet garni

Note You may find you also have to sew up any gashes in the skin. Since the bird is to be stuffed tightly, there must not be any holes or the stuffing will all fall out. It is always better to have too much stuffing than too little as an understuffed bird will just look mean.

Lay the bird out on a board. It will be easier to deal with if there is just one big cut down the backbone that can be sewn up after you have stuffed it. Line the inside of the bird with a layer of the forcemeat, veal or sausage meat. Lay some strips of ham and bacon over the forcemeat, interspersed with the pistachio nuts and truffle or mushroom slices. Season these well and cover them with another layer of forcemeat. Continue like this until all the ingredients are used up, remembering that when the bird is served, it will be cut across and will look like a pâté so make sure the ingredients are evenly distributed. Remember too that the skin will have to meet to be sewn up so do not get too enthusiastic – try to keep the shape of the bird in mind as you stuff it.

When the bird is full, pull the edges together and sew up firmly. Soyer ties his poussin firmly in a napkin (cheesecloth or alternative) and poaches it for approximately 1 hour in a good veal or chicken stock, with a few carrots, an onion and a bouquet garni. He then cools and weights it in the stock and serves it garnished with chopped aspic. Although it is less authentic, I prefer to coat the skin of the bird with plenty of butter, cover its breast with a little foil, and roast it in a well-buttered baking pan, sewn side down, at 350°, allowing 20 minutes per pound. Fifteen minutes before it is cooked, remove the foil and baste the bird well so that it has a good brown top. The bird then only needs to be cooled and chilled thoroughly before slicing.

FORCEMEAT OF VEAL

INGREDIENTS

*1 cup well trimmed, very finely ground
   lean veal
²⁄₃ cup ground beef suet
²⁄₃ cup water
1 tablespoon butter
½ cup all-purpose flour
3 eggs
salt and pepper
pinch of nutmeg*

Mix the veal with the suet. Put the water in a pan with the butter and when it is boiling, stir in the flour. Continue to stir over the heat until it forms a "smooth and toughish paste," then remove from the heat and beat it into the veal and suet mixture. Add one whole egg and season generously with the salt, pepper and nutmeg. Separate the other eggs and beat the yolks into the forcemeat. Whip the whites until they hold their shape, then fold them too into the forcemeat.

CHAMPIGNONS EN SURPRISE
Serves 8

Meringue mushrooms would certainly have appealed to Soyer's sense of fun and will perk up the most jaded appetite at the end of a long – if delicious – meal. They are very easy to make and store well, so it might be worth making double the quantity for future occasions.

INGREDIENTS

*2–3 egg whites
½ cup extra-fine sugar
2–4 oz good quality semi-sweet
   chocolate
1¼ cups heavy cream
sugar
2 tablespoons brandy or liqueur*

Cover two baking sheets with some foil or brown paper. Put two of the egg whites in a bowl and whip them till they are really stiff. Add the sugar and continue to whip until the mixture is very shiny and holds its shape in sharp peaks. Fill into a piping bag fitted with a large round tip. Pipe eight disks, about 2 inches in diameter, for the caps of the mushrooms on to one of the baking sheets. Then pipe eight "stalks," not more than 1½ inches long, on to the other baking sheet. Grate the chocolate finely but generously over the mushroom caps and bake both caps and stalks at 200° for about 2 hours, or until they are quite set.

Carefully pry the caps and stalks off the paper. With a sharp knife, scoop out a hole in the underside of each mushroom cap to allow the stalk to slot in. Paint the hole and the bottom of each stalk with egg white and fit them together carefully. Replace them on the baking sheets and put them in the oven for another 30 minutes to set the egg white "glue." Remove the mushrooms very carefully and store in a box until you are ready to use them.

To make the cream, whip the heavy cream lightly with a little sugar, until it holds its shape. Gently fold in a couple of tablespoons of brandy or a liqueur of your choice. If you want to achieve a lighter effect, whip the remaining egg white until it holds its shape in soft peaks, then fold it into the cream. Pile the whipped cream in the center of a decorative serving dish with the mushrooms arranged around the outside.

GELEE DE FRUITS MARBRE
Serves 8 if offered with other desserts, 4 to 6 on its own

The Victorians loved to make trick jellies and creams that allowed you to "look" through a clear jelly "wall" into a decorated cream inside. They used highly ornate double molds to set the outside jelly before filling it with the cream. In the absence of such a gadget, you can use two mixing bowls, one just slightly smaller than the other, and compensate for the lack of twirls and whirls on your mold with artistic, fruity decorations. Soyer's Gelée was flavored with Maraschino, a sweet liqueur made from the kernel of the Marasca cherry, and much favored by Victorian ladies. You can, however, substitute any fruit liqueur and choose a complementary fruity decoration. The Gelée can be made the day before you need it, although I would not recommend unmolding it until just before the meal.

INGREDIENTS

1 envelope gelatin
1 cup hot water
⅔ cup fruit liqueur
fruit to decorate the inside of the jelly
3 large egg yolks
3 tablespoons extra-fine sugar
1 cup warmed milk
½ cup heavy cream

Melt half the gelatin in half the water. Gradually add the remaining water and ¼ cup of the liqueur and allow to cool. Using sunflower or some other very light-tasting oil, oil the inside of a 1 quart bowl or mold and the outside of a 1¼ pint bowl or mold lightly. Pour the jelly mixture into the large bowl. Put the smaller bowl inside and fill with tins or weights until the jelly rises up the sides of the inner bowl. (You are trying to achieve an even and reasonably thin layer of jelly between the bowls.) Put the bowls in a refrigerator to chill, making sure that they do not move as you carry them. When the jelly is absolutely set, remove the weights and pour a little boiling water into the inside bowl. Swish it around for a minute, then discard it. This should be enough to loosen the inside bowl but if it is not, repeat the process until you can pry out the inside bowl with the tip of a knife. Put the outside bowl back in the refrigerator to re-chill for a few minutes.

Meanwhile slice the fruit very thinly and use it to decorate the inside of the bowl in as ornate a pattern as you can invent.

Put the egg yolks in a heavy pan or a double boiler and stir in the sugar briskly. Over a very low heat and stirring continuously, add the warmed milk gradually and cook gently until the custard thickens slightly, then remove it from the heat – take care not to let it boil and thus curdle. Melt the remaining gelatin in the remaining liqueur and stir into the custard. Leave until it is quite cool. Whip the cream with a balloon whisk lightly until it just holds its shape, then fold it into the custard. With a large spoon or ladle, spoon the custard mixture carefully into the jelly, taking care not to dislodge the fruit decoration. Put in the refrigerator for 2 hours to chill and set thoroughly.

To serve, dip the outer bowl briefly in hot water and unmold on to a decorative serving dish – the oil should make it turn out fairly easily.

CROQUETTES DE MACARONI AU FROMAGE DE STILTON
Serves 8

I find that blue Stilton has slightly too strong a flavor when cooked so I prefer to use white, but this is simply a matter of personal taste. Soyer does not specify which color he wishes used and since both were available in the 19th century, either would be historically correct.

You can make the croquettes in advance and reheat them for 20 minutes in a moderately hot oven, or, ideally, in a combination microwave and convection oven with the convection oven at about 400° and the microwave on low for 10 minutes – this heats the inside of the croquettes without drying them while crisping up the bread crumb coating.

INGREDIENTS

1 cup small macaroni
1⅓ tablespoons butter
2⅓ tablespoons all-purpose flour
2 cups whole creamy milk
2 cups grated blue or white Stilton
salt and pepper
cayenne
grated nutmeg
3 egg yolks
1 large, whole egg, beaten
2 generous handfuls of fresh brown
  bread crumbs
oil for deep frying

Cook the macaroni in plenty of boiling water until it is soft but still *al dente,* then drain it quickly and return it to the pan to keep warm. Meanwhile, melt the butter in another pan and add the flour; stir for a few minutes to cook the roux, then add the milk gradually. Continue to cook and stir until the sauce thickens slightly. Add the macaroni, grated cheese and seasonings

GELEE DE FRUITS MARBRE AND CROQUETTES DE MACARONI AU FROMAGE DE STILTON

to taste. Then add the egg yolks and cook for a further few minutes to allow the egg yolks to set. Remove the pan from the heat and leave the mixture to get completely cold in the pan – it will then be easier to handle.

When you are ready to make the croquettes, use a large teaspoon to shape ovals out of the mixture. Coat each croquette with the beaten egg and then, generously, with the bread crumbs. Heat the oil in a deep pan, place the croquettes in a frying basket and fry for 2 to 3 minutes, depending on size. They should be brown and crisp on the outside but not burned. Drain on paper towels and serve immediately, or reserve to be reheated when they are needed. Soyer says to "dress them in a pyramid, upon a napkin, and serve very hot."

CANNING AND PRESERVING

Before the Victorian era, the techniques of food preservation had changed little over many centuries. Salting, pickling, drying and smoking of meats and fishes had all been practiced since Saxon times. The exclusion of air (contact with which was thought to be the sole cause of spoiling) by sealing with melted butter or lard, the use of sugar to preserve fruits, and the sun-drying of certain fruits and vegetables had also proved reliable ways of keeping foods edible for quite long periods.

In the 18th century successful experiments had been carried out with "dried soups." These were made by reducing meat stocks to a "glue" that could be reconstituted when needed. Such glues formed a staple item among ships' stores for several decades although they never attained much popularity outside the navy.

Throughout the 19th century experiments were also conducted in preserving meat chemically. Although some of them were moderately successful, they were soon overtaken by the more efficient techniques of canning and, eventually, freezing. However, by the 1880s a greater understanding of Pasteur's theories on disease and putrefaction led scientists to experiment further with chemicals in an attempt to kill the germs or bacteria in foodstuffs. From 1880 onwards several strongly preservative chemicals (formaldehyde, borates, silicates and sulphites) were being added quite indiscriminately to food. They certainly killed the bacteria, but it was soon realized that many of them could have the same effect on the people who ate the food. As the result of widespread uneasiness, particularly about the formalin (used to keep milk fresh), which was thought to cause inflammation of the stomach, the government appointed a committee in 1899 to look into the matter. Its report in 1901 was followed by legislation to control the use of chemical preservatives in food.

A Frenchman, Nicholas Appert, was the first person to prove, at the end of the 18th century, that foods could be successfully preserved by sealing in glass bottles and then heating. The next discovery was made by an Englishman, Bryan Donkin, a partner in a foundry, who realized, to the considerable profit of his company, that Appert's techniques could also be applied to tinned containers. By 1812 a factory had been built and in 1818, between January and September alone, the Admiralty purchased 23,779 canisters of canned foods. Donkin packed meat, vegetables and soup into his cans and although they were more expensive than fresh food, the navy found them highly satisfactory. Whether it was due to their cost, the difficulty of opening them (Donkin's cans bore the instructions: "Cut round the top round the outer edge with a chisel and hammer") or just natural conservatism, the cans do not appear to have had much sale outside naval circles.

By the 1830s and 1840s several other firms had sprung up, also supplying mainly naval outlets. However, a scandal in 1850, when it was discovered that a large proportion of the canned meat supplied by one Stephen Goldner was putrid, did immense harm to the industry. What had actually happened was that Goldner had started to pack his meat into larger and larger canisters, but had heated these no longer than the smaller ones. Whereas the heat had been sufficient to penetrate a can filled with 3–6 pounds of meat and kill the bacteria, it was not sufficient to penetrate 9–14 pounds with the result that bacteria were not destroyed and the meat went bad. Since both canners and scientists still believed successful canning depended solely on the exclusion of all air from the cans, they did not understand what had happened. The resulting public suspicion of canned meat did not subside until the late 1860s and 1870s.

The problem of how to heat the cans successfully was one with which canners battled throughout the century. The solution was eventually found in an "autoclave" – a closed vessel containing pressurized steam. The risk of a can exploding under pressure was reduced by the fact that the pressure inside and outside the can in the autoclave was similar, while the autoclaves were fitted with meters and safety valves to minimize the risk of their exploding.

By the 1860s canned meat was being imported in bulk from Australia and America – twenty-two million pounds of it by 1871. Its main – possibly only – virtue was that it was very cheap. Certainly, if this contemporary description was accurate, it was not appetizing:

"It was in *big*, thick, clumsy red tins . . . I have a vivid recollection of the unappetising look of the contents – a large lump of coarse-grained lean meat inclined to separate into coarse fibres, a large lump of unpleasant-looking fat on one side of it – and an irregular hollow partly filled with watery fluid."

Frozen meat, introduced in the 1880s, quickly supplanted the less attractive canned variety, but by that time the convenience of canning as a method of long-term storage for many foods had become well established. How to open the cans did remain a problem though. Openers and "easy-open" cans proliferated during the closing years of the century, none of them really successful. Not that the 20th century has done much better – most of the can openers available today are based on Victorian patents.

Efforts to crack the problem of refrigeration were made throughout the 19th century. It had long been known that freezing foods would keep them in excellent condition – the question was how to make or keep enough ice. In the 1820s George Dempster, a London fishmonger, was shipping salmon from Scotland packed in ice, and later in the century, an enterprising American is said to have found it worth shipping ice from Boston to Cape Town in order to bring back fresh grapes, but in mass terms, the cost was prohibitive.

The answer was to invent an ice-making machine but this proved more difficult than originally anticipated. The first machines were made in 1850 by a Scottish-Australian emigrant, James Harrison. They were based on ether, which produces a fall in temperature as it evaporates. Two French brothers, Edmund and Ferdinand Carré, then found that compressed

TINNED PROVISIONS, INCLUDING FISH, MEAT, GAME, FRUIT AND
HOUSEHOLD REQUISITES.

ammonia gas was a cheaper and more efficient refrigerant. This was to become the basis for all land-based refrigeration plants until the introduction of carbon dioxide in the 1890s. However, they were still a long way from being able to freeze meat to travel the thirteen thousand sea miles from Australia to England, as operating any of their processes on board ship proved almost impossible. Experiments with cooled brine and gas continued for the next thirty years without success. Finally, a system using chilled air was devised and in 1880 the first successfully chilled cargo of meat arrived from Australia on board the SS *Strathleven*. From then on a continuous trade in chilled meat was established, its quality soon forcing the less attractive canned meat off the shelves.

CHAPTER FOUR

MISS ELIZA ACTON'S "MODERN DINNER FOR A PRIVATE FAMILY"

F ew people know much about Eliza Acton other than the fact that her publisher, Thomas Longman, rejected her slim volumes of sentimental verse, telling her to write a cookbook instead. In fact, not a great deal more is known of her life, although much can be deduced about her character from the many editions of her *Modern Cookery* and her excellent *Bread Book*.

We do know that she was born in 1799, the daughter of an Ipswich brewer. We also know that she was "delicate" as a young girl and, for the sake of her health, was sent to France, where she became engaged to a French officer and, presumably, developed her interest in French cookery. The interest in French cookery lasted; the engagement did not. However, it was later rumored that the girl whom Eliza called her niece and who spent a lot of time with her was in fact her own illegitimate daughter, so maybe the French officer also left his mark. It is certain that Eliza never married, although she maintained her own establishment in Hampstead. Despite her "delicacy" she survived to the relatively ripe old age of sixty.

That she was sensible, practical, with a scientific turn of mind and a remarkably happy way with English prose if not poetry, is obvious from a quick glance at the Preface to *Modern Cookery*. Eliza was middle class herself and wrote for the middle class. She expected her readers to employ a cook, but did not expect them to be blessed with large incomes; hence her constant concern about economy and her detestation of waste. By the time she revised *Modern Cookery* in 1855, she had become aware of the dire poverty in which so many of her countrymen lived and the appalling fact that much of the food they could afford had been adulterated, to such a degree that it was actually poisonous.

The writings of Baron Leibig and other early nutritionists confirmed Eliza's instinctive belief in the importance of wholesome ingredients for the maintenance of good health. Her *English Bread Book* (published in 1852 for four shillings and sixpence) not only contains analyses of all the latest research but makes it quite clear that she had visited the lethal bakery shops where alum was added to bread in almost equal quantities to flour. Hence her "ample directions for making what cannot be purchased in this country – unadulterated bread of the most undeniably wholesome quality." Nor was bread the only object of her concern. The same passage continues: ". . . also ample directions for those refreshing and finely flavoured varieties of preserved fruit which are so seductive to health when judiciously taken . . . many of those made up for sale being absolutely dangerous eating; those which are not adulterated generally so oversweetened as to be distasteful . . ."

From this one might suspect that Eliza would not countenance "foreign fripperies;" this was far from the case. Her early experiences in France had given her great respect for the frugality and nutritional content of traditional French cooking. Therefore, although she saw no virtue in "blindly adopting foreign modes in anything merely because they *are* foreign," she was most anxious "to learn from other nations who excel us in aught good or useful and," she goes on,

OPPOSITE: BORDYKE VEAL CAKE AND "AN EXCELLENT SALAD OF YOUNG VEGETABLES"

"whose greater frugality, combined with almost universal culinary skill, or culinary knowledge at the least is well worth our imitation."

To this end, *Modern Cookery* contains recipes for every aspect of cooking: soups, sauces and gravies, fish, salads and vegetables, meats of all kinds, boiled and roasted, pastries, soufflés and omelettes, boiled and baked puddings, sweet dishes, preserves and pickles, cakes (although she thoroughly disapproves of them as being indigestible and fattening), confectionery, syrups and drinks, and, of course, home made bread. Although this is what we would expect of a comprehensive cookbook today, none of her contemporaries even attempted it.

Not only is there an abundance of recipes but they are all laid out clearly and comprehensibly (Eliza was the first food writer ever to give a list of ingredients with quantities at the bottom of each recipe and an idea of how long the dish would take to cook). There are also detailed instructions as to the technicalities of cooking: boning, trussing and carving meats and poultry, thickening sauces, persuading the much despised cakes to rise, glazing or "icing" pastry and so on. And, what is almost (*pace* Dr. Kitchiner) unheard of at her time, she tested all her own recipes in her own kitchen:

". . . our receipts are such as can be *perfectly depended on* from having been proved beneath our own roof . . . We have trusted nothing to others; but having desired sincerely to render the work one of general usefulness, we have spared neither cost nor labour to make it so."

When so much work, skill and knowledge went into *Modern Cookery,* it seems particularly unfair that it should have been plagiarized, stolen from and appropriated by other writers so extensively, even during her lifetime, to such a degree that, in the revised edition that came out in 1855, Eliza appended "Author's Receipt" and "Author's Original Receipt" to many of the recipes in an attempt to prevent such pilferage. It seems even more unjust that since the 1868 edition, the book has only been reprinted, and then not in its entirety, three times whereas Isabella Beeton's *Household Management,* which contains many of Eliza's recipes (unacknowledged), has never been out of print since the 1860s. Today, however, Eliza's seminal influence on English cookery is fully recognized and appreciated – and her recipes are back in use.

GRAVY SOUP

Serves 8

A "rich, old-fashioned English brown gravy-soup" Eliza calls this, and rich it certainly is. However, the flavor is delicious and the discarded meat and vegetables make an excellent basis for a "cottage pie."

INGREDIENTS

about 4½ lb stewing beef, well trimmed
4 tablespoons seasoned whole-wheat flour
6 tablespoons butter
2 fairly large onions, roughly chopped
4 carrots, diced
4 turnips, diced
4 celery stalks, chopped
4 bouquets garnis
10 cloves
4 blades of mace or 1 teaspoon ground mace
15 peppercorns
2 quarts water
5 tablespoons whole-wheat flour
1 tablespoon soy sauce
1¼ cups medium sweet sherry
cayenne

Toss the beef in the seasoned flour. Melt 4 tablespoons of the butter in a large, heavy pan, add the onions and the beef and fry briskly for 5 to 10 minutes, or until they are all brown without being burned. Add the carrots, turnips and celery, the herbs and spices and the water. Bring to a boil slowly and simmer gently for at least 3 hours. Alternatively use a slow cookpot overnight. Strain the soup, discarding or reserving the beef and vegetables for another dish, and leave it to cool completely.

Remove any excess fat and reheat the soup. Rub the flour into the remaining butter, add a little of the hot soup to make a thin paste, then return the paste to the soup pan. Cook for 5 minutes, stirring continuously, until the soup thickens slightly. Remove from the heat and add the soy sauce, sherry and a generous pinch of cayenne. Taste and add further salt or pepper if you think it is necessary before serving. Do not allow the soup to boil or you will lose the full flavor of the sherry.

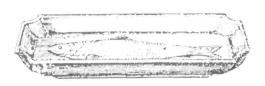

BAKED SOLES

Serves 8

"A simple but excellent receipt . . . Fresh large soles, dressed in the following manner, are remarkably tender and delicate eating; much more so than those which are fried . . . the difference between them was very marked, especially as regards the exceeding tenderness of the flesh." And they are less trouble to cook . . .

INGREDIENTS

8 soles, cleaned but on the bone
8 tablespoons fine brown bread crumbs
generous pinch of salt and white pepper
generous pinch of cayenne
generous pinch of mace
generous pinch of nutmeg
1 cup butter, just melted but not boiled
1 large egg

Wash and thoroughly dry the fish. Season the bread crumbs with the salt, pepper and spices. Mix about 2½ tablespoons of the butter with the egg and brush the soles generously with this mixture, then sprinkle the fish lavishly with most of the bread crumbs. Press these down firmly on each fish with the back of a broad-bladed knife. Pour a little of the melted butter over the bottom of as many flat, ovenproof dishes as will be needed to hold all the sole, then lift the fish carefully into them with a slice. Pour the rest of the butter over the fish slowly and sprinkle the remaining bread crumbs on top. Bake the fish, uncovered, at 350° for 30 minutes. Serve immediately with a green vegetable or salad.

If you want to serve the soles filleted, remove them from the dishes carefully before serving, fillet them, trying not to disrupt the crisp crumb topping more than you have to, and rearrange them on individual warmed plates.

BORDYKE VEAL CAKE

Serves 10

This recipe has "Good" after it in brackets and Eliza goes on to add that it is "excellent cold" – a high recommendation. I have been unable to locate Bordyke, although it sounds as if it should be in the Lake District. Because of the amount of bacon I did not think any further salt was needed but if you like your food well salted, add a little.

INGREDIENTS

1½ lb well trimmed stewing veal
(about 2 lb untrimmed)
½ lb lean bacon
grated rind of 2 small lemons
½ teaspoon mace
¼ teaspoon cayenne

Grind the veal coarsely with the bacon, then mix in the lemon rind and spices thoroughly. Press the mixture into a loaf pan (the base lined with wax paper or foil to prevent sticking) – it should come three quarters of the way up the sides – and leave it slightly mounded in the middle. Bake at 350° for 45 minutes. Eliza tells you to remove the cake immediately from the pan and to cool it on a rack "that the fat may drain from it." These days it is less fat than water with which our meat is filled, so you may need to remove the veal cake from the pan to drain off excess liquid. In either case, leave it to cool completely, then serve with a good salad and boiled or baked potatoes.

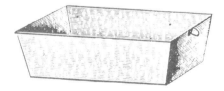

ROAST FOWL – A FRENCH RECEIPT

Serves 6 to 8

For anyone who likes either butter or lemon, this is quite the most delicious way of roasting a chicken.

INGREDIENTS

1 large chicken or capon, with giblets
1 onion
1 carrot
1 celery stalk
1 turnip
2 parsley stalks
2½ cups fresh brown bread crumbs
finely grated rind and juice of 1 lemon
3 tablespoons very finely chopped
*   parsley*
1 teaspoon fresh or dried thyme
½ teaspoon salt
generous pinch of nutmeg
generous pinch of black pepper
1 stick butter
1 egg yolk
1 tablespoon whole-wheat flour

Put the giblets of the chicken into a pan with the vegetables, parsley stalks and about 2 cups water or water with a dash of white wine. Bring to the boil and simmer for 30 minutes, then strain.

Mix 2 cups of the bread crumbs with half the lemon rind, 1 tablespoon of the parsley, the thyme, salt, nutmeg and pepper. Melt half the butter and add it to the mixture with the egg yolk. Work it all together well with your hands and stuff it into the body or breast of the bird, as you prefer.

Roast the chicken at 350°, allowing 20 minutes per pound plus an extra 20 minutes. Thirty minutes before the chicken is cooked, remove it from the oven and drain off any excess fat from the baking pan. Mix the remaining bread crumbs with the remaining lemon rind and melt the remaining butter. Pour some butter over the chicken, then sprinkle it with some of the bread crumb mixture. Pour a little more butter on, then a few more crumbs until all are used up. Return the chicken to the oven to finish cooking.

When the bird is cooked, transfer it to a serving dish and keep it warm. Add the flour to the buttery juices in the baking pan, stir over a low heat until the flour is cooked, then add about 1¼ cups of the chicken stock slowly. Stir and cook until the sauce thickens slightly. Add the lemon juice and remaining parsley and a little more seasoning if necessary. Serve the sauce piping hot with the chicken.

POTATO RIBBONS

Serves 8

These are quite delicious, "pre-packet" potato chips, but they are fiddly to make. Ideally you should peel large potatoes, cut them in thick slices, then pare each slice round into a ribbon – which is feasible but very slow. A quicker way to achieve short ribbons would be to slice large potatoes very thinly on a mandolin and then cut the slices into ribbons. Whichever you decide to do, the slices must be paper-thin to achieve the proper crisp effect. Eliza deep fried her ribbons in butter, which is delicious but very expensive; a good light vegetable oil such as sunflower works equally well.

INGREDIENTS

1 lb potatoes, peeled
1½ lb butter or 3¾ cups vegetable oil
fine sea salt (optional)
cayenne (optional)

Slice the potatoes into thin ribbons (see above) and dry them lightly. Heat the butter or oil in a deep frying pan until a bread cube sizzles when dropped in. Using a basket or perforated spoon, lower the potato ribbons gently into the fat or oil in fairly small quantities. Fry them briskly for a minute or two, taking care they do not burn. Remove them and drain on paper towels. Serve lightly sprinkled with salt and cayenne, if liked. The potatoes are good both hot and cold; they can be made in advance and reheated in a moderate oven for 5 to 10 minutes.

OPPOSITE: ROAST FOWL – A FRENCH
RECEIPT – AND POTATO RIBBONS

CARROTS IN THEIR OWN JUICE

Serves 8

"By the following mode of dressing carrots," says Eliza, "whether they be young or old, their full flavour and all the nutriment they contain are entirely preserved; and they are at the same time rendered so palatable with it that they furnish at once an admirable dish to eat without meat as well as with it. A simple but excellent receipt."

INGREDIENTS

2 lb carrots, peeled and trimmed
2 tablespoons butter
1/4 cup all-purpose flour
handful of parsley, coarsely chopped
1/3 cup heavy cream
juice of 1 orange
salt and freshly ground black pepper

Slice the carrots thinly, then put them into enough boiling, salted water to cover them and cook until tender, about 15 to 20 minutes. Meanwhile, soften the butter in a largish bowl and mix it with the flour, parsley and cream. Drain the carrots, reserving 1 cup of their cooking water. Add this liquid to the butter and cream mixture, stirring well to keep it smooth. Add the carrots and return to the saucepan. Cook for 2 minutes to thicken the sauce. Add the orange juice and black pepper, adjust the seasoning to taste and serve immediately.

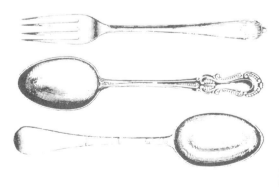

"AN EXCELLENT SALAD OF YOUNG VEGETABLES"

Serves 8

Excellent indeed, especially with her equally excellent Bordyke Veal Cake (page 53).

INGREDIENTS

about 24 cooked artichoke hearts,
    sliced – these can be canned (3 1/2 lb
    cans) or frozen (2 lb)
1 1/4 lb potatoes, scrubbed, then boiled
    or steamed and sliced
1 lb young carrots, scrubbed, then
    boiled or steamed and sliced
2 tablespoons chopped fresh herbs such
    as chives or thyme or a mixture of
    several
8 tablespoons good French dressing

Arrange the sliced artichoke hearts in the bottom of a wide dish. Cover them with the potato slices, then the carrot slices. Sprinkle the fresh herbs over them all and add the French dressing, just before the salad is to be served.

COMPOTE OF SPRING FRUIT

Serves 8

"We would *especially* recommend these delicate and very agreeable preparations for trial to such of our readers as may be unacquainted with them, as well as to those who may have a distaste to the common *stewed fruit* of English cookery. If well made they are peculiarly delicious and refreshing, preserving the pure flavour of the fruit of which they are composed . . . They are more economical than tarts or puddings, and infinitely more wholesome . . . The syrup can be enriched with a larger quantity [of sugar] when they are intended for the desserts of formal dinners, as it will increase the transparency of the fruit; the juice is always beautifully clear when the *compôtes* are carefully prepared." With such a recommendation, how can they fail? Compotes can be made of any soft fruit, the amount of sugar being adjusted to the tartness of the fruit.

INGREDIENTS

*3 lb fresh young rhubarb, trimmed and
wiped
2 cups water
½ cup extra-fine sugar*

Cut the rhubarb, diagonally, into large pieces. Meanwhile, melt the sugar in the water and boil it gently for 10 minutes. Add the rhubarb and continue to cook gently for a further 10 to 12 minutes, turning the rhubarb very carefully (so as to leave the stems intact) after 5 minutes to make sure it is evenly cooked. Turn into a serving dish, preferably glass, and serve with cream.

YOUNG WIFE'S PUDDING
Serves 8

Eliza gives "minute directions" for this pudding because "although it is very simple, it is delicate and good" – and presumably not beyond the capabilities of a young wife. However, great care must be taken not to cook it too fast or all will be ruined.

INGREDIENTS

*6 egg yolks and 4 egg whites
about ⅓ cup extra-fine sugar
grated rind of 1½ lemons
3 cups whole milk
¾ cup heavy cream
3–4 thin slices of fine whole-wheat
bread, buttered thickly on one side
only*

Beat the egg yolks and whites in a bowl with a fork, then add ¼ cup of the sugar, the lemon rind, milk and cream. Mix well, then pour into a decorative but ovenproof flan or pie dish. Lay the buttered bread, butter side up, on the top of the pudding (it will float) and sprinkle it generously with the remaining sugar. Put the dish into a *bain marie* and cook it at 250° for at least 1 hour, by which time it should be just set. Serve warm or cold with extra cream.

VERMICELLI PUDDING
Serves 8

Vermicelli was often used for sweet dishes in the 18th and 19th centuries and combined with the apples it makes, as Eliza says, "an exceedingly nice pudding – if well made and well baked . . ."

INGREDIENTS

*1½ lb cooking apples or tart eating
apples, peeled
5 cups milk
4 oz vermicelli
4 tablespoons butter
⅓ cup extra-fine sugar
4 large eggs
grated rind and juice of 1 lemon*

Cut the apples into thick, even slices. Use half of them to line a well-buttered 1½ quart baking dish. Bring the milk to a boil in a pan, then gently break in the vermicelli, stirring all the time with a wooden spoon to prevent it sticking. Cook gently for 15 to 20 minutes, or till the vermicelli is quite soft, stirring regularly. Remove the pan from the heat and work in the butter and the sugar gently. Beat the eggs with a fork and stir them into the vermicelli mixture with the lemon rind and juice.

Spoon the mixture into the baking dish and cover with the remaining apples, arranged in a pattern. Press each slice down into the pudding, then let it bob back. Bake the pudding at 250° for 45 minutes, or until it is just set. Serve warm with extra cream if you like.

OVERLEAF: COMPOTE OF SPRING FRUIT
(LEFT) VERMICELLI PUDDING (TOP LEFT)
AND YOUNG WIFE'S PUDDING

MASS ADULTERATION OF FOODSTUFFS

The early years of the 19th century saw appalling levels of food adulteration but many of the practices used by the bakers, brewers, coffee and tea merchants, cheesemakers, confectionery manufacturers and so on had originated in the previous century. Although most trades were subject to regulations and offenders were prosecuted and fined, the sums were relatively small and had little effect. The public were first made aware of the dangers by a German chemist called Frederick Accum who, in 1820, published a long, reasoned, detailed and scientifically correct report on the misdeeds of the manufacturers. Not only did he expose their frauds, but he published lists of those druggists, grocers, brewers and so on who had been convicted and fined for adulteration of their goods.

Accum's *Treatise on the Adulterations of Food and Culinary Poisons* not only aroused deep concern amongst the public, but also fierce resentment and opposition among the traders he had exposed. He was subjected to a violent and vindictive public attack and finally indicted on the trivial – and never proven – charge that he had defaced some of the Royal Institution's books by removing spare leaves. Such was the power of the opposition that Accum's reputation was ruined, rather than face prosecution he retired to Germany. Moreover, his work was discredited and public alarm died down. Periodic reports continued to be made over the next twenty years, but it was not until 1850 that *The Lancet,* a respected medical journal, took up the challenge and appointed an Analytical and Sanitary Commission "to inquire into and report on the quality of the solids and fluids consumed by all classes of the public." The commissioners only numbered two – Dr. Hassall who was responsible for the chemical analysis, and Dr. Letheby, an authority on diet – but their influence was far reaching.

Basically, Hassall's findings confirmed all of Accum's accusations: wine was made from spoiled cider; "crusted port" was made by lining bottles with "supertartarate of potash;" poisonous "cocculus indicus," liquorice, salts of steel and molasses were used in the manufacture of beer; blackthorn leaves were sold instead of tea; cheese was colored with red lead; all bread was filled with illegal quantities of alum; confectionery was colored with poisonous salts of copper and lead; cheap rancid butter was washed in milk, sweetened and passed off as best Epping butter, and so on and so on.

By 1855 the *Lancet*'s investigations had caused sufficient concern for the appointment of a Select Parliamentary Commission which, in turn, led to the passing of the first Food and Drugs Act in 1860. However, the adulterators were not quite finished, as the new act was administered with little enthusiasm. It was not until it was comprehensively revised in 1872 and the appointment of public food analysts came under the control of the local police forces that any genuine improvement took place.

Meanwhile, the steadily growing populations of the larger cities presented their own problems. One of the most serious, and long standing, was the need to provide a regular supply of clean water. Until the middle of the 19th century, water closets were virtually unknown and sewage disposal was a constant problem. By the middle of the century, London had over two hundred and fifty thousand cesspools, many of which still drained into the Thames. Water sources were scarce and frequently polluted, greatly increasing the risk of cholera and other water-borne diseases.

As early as 1837 a scientist called Chadwick and the Unitarian minister, Southwood Smith, were pressing for investigations into the effects of bad sanitation on the health of the citizens of the larger towns. Chemical analysis of the water,

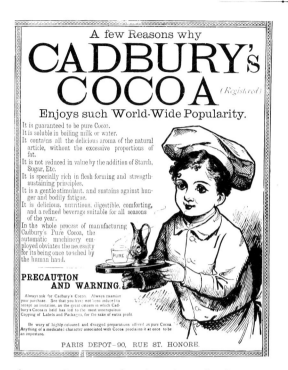

the appointment of various investigating commissions and, finally, the appointment of Sir John Simon as Medical Officer for London in 1848 all contributed to the disappearance of the "privy bucket" system of sewage disposal and the creation of enclosed, underground sewers.

Milk presented another problem in cities too large for it to be brought from the nearby countryside. City cows were kept in appalling conditions:

"Two in each seven feet of space . . . no ventilation, save by a tile roof through which the ammoniacal vapours escape . . . Besides the animals there is . . . a large tank for grains and hay, and between them a receptacle into which the liquid manure drains and the solid is heaped . . . the stench thence arising is insufferable."

Hardly surprisingly, the milk the cows gave was thin and often contaminated. The situation was greatly improved by the arrival of the railways which could transport milk from the distant countryside quickly and hygienically. An epidemic in the 1860s wiped out many of the cities' cattle, and they were not replaced.

The railroads made a similarly positive contribution to the supply of fresh meat and fish to the cities. Fresh fish had always presented so great a problem that the majority of what was sold in the cities was salted or pickled. However the combined effect of the new steam trawlers that could return a catch to land at relatively great speed, and the railroads that could transport it, changed the picture rapidly.

Public awareness of the deleterious effect of eating diseased or tainted meats was dramatically heightened by various reports during the 1840s and 1850s. As a result, the municipal authorities both tightened and vigorously enforced the restrictions governing the inspection of meat markets and merchants. From the middle of the century too the lower end of the market was supplied with cheap and relatively wholesome, if unappetizing, canned meat from Australia and America.

Bread was the other commodity to be strikingly affected by the inventions of the 19th century. The long standing if unwholesome desire of the public for white bread, and the need of the millers and bakers for a flour that would keep, led to much experimentation with roller rather than grinding mills. Not only were roller mills cheaper to maintain and easier to operate, but they ground the flour fine enough to flatten the wheat germ in the grain so that it could be sifted off with the bran. Since it was the wheat germ that not only provided the maximum nutrition but, because of its natural oils, caused the flour to go rancid, its disappearance produced a whiter flour that kept longer. Both baker and customer had achieved their desires.

MRS. BEETON'S "HOUSEHOLD MANAGEMENT"

Although in the four years between the publication of *The Book of Household Management* in 1861 and Isabella Beeton's death, her book had been gratifyingly successful – not a blockbuster in modern terms, but selling steadily and well – no one would have been more surprised than she to learn that a hundred years later it would have become the bible of the 20th-century cook.

Why it should have been so much more successful than so many contemporary works is still somewhat of a mystery. It was undoubtedly the most comprehensive such book to be published at that time. Not only did it provide recipes and menus, but it also included information and advice on marketing, seasonality, the costs and origins of foods, housekeeping, the management of servants, medicine and law. It also had full color plates – something that none of its contemporaries could boast. Its recipes were down to earth, fairly easy to follow and pretty reliable, appealing to the growing middle classes, who still buy her book today. The phenomenal long-term success of the book may, however, be due in part to the publishers, Ward, Lock and Tyler (now just Ward Lock). They acquired the rights to *The Book of Household Management* along with Sam Beeton and all his works in 1866, a year after his wife's death, when his empire was brought down by the ruin of his financiers, Overend, Gurney and Co. Building on the success that the book had already had, the publishers ensured that it was regularly updated, reprinted and promoted until it had acquired

a momentum of its own.

In fact, *The Book of Household Management* was the culmination of the "magazine" trend in cookery writing that had got under way in the 1850s when most of the taxes previously levied on all forms of printing were removed. The result was an explosion of magazines and cheap "parts works," fueled by the industrialization of the printing presses and the expansion of the railroads, enabling their products to be distributed quickly and cheaply throughout the country.

Sam Beeton was at the forefront of this development. He had founded his success in the early 1850s on the publication of Harriet Beecher Stowe's classic, *Uncle Tom's Cabin*. This was followed over the next fifteen years by *The Englishwoman's Domestic Magazine*, the *Boy's Own Journal*, *The Dictionary of Universal Information*, *The Queen* and *The Moniteur du Monde* (both fashion journals), *Beeton's Illustrated Bible*, *The Book of Household Management* and *Wild Sport of the World*, to mention only the most successful. Most of Sam's publications started as magazines, then sold in "parts" (one chapter each month so that you could gradually collect the whole work, then buy a binder to keep it in), and finally in bound form. This is certainly how *The Book of Household Management* came out, originally as monthly supplements to the *Englishwoman's Domestic Magazine* and then as a bound book.

Sam and Isabella Beeton formed such a very close professional partnership that it is not always easy to see where one's work started and the other's stopped. From soon after their marriage in 1856, Isabella took an active part in Sam's publishing business: editing and writing articles for the *Englishwoman's Domestic Magazine*, choosing plates for fashion articles or thinking

OPPOSITE: SALMON A LA GENEVESE (TOP), CELERY A LA CREME (LEFT) AND STEWED BELGIAN ENDIVE

up schemes for mail order paper patterns to be sold through the magazines. *The Book of Household Management,* however, was entirely her idea and, in the main, her production. Sam's contributions were the asides and bons mots in almost every entry, most of which came from his *Dictionary of Universal Knowledge* on which he was hard at work at the time.

In the fashion of the magazine era, Isabella intended her book to be a compilation of readers' recipes, edited and amplified by herself. But, although they appealed for recipes through the magazine and actually received several thousand, most of them proved thoroughly unsatisfactory so Isabella turned instead to the classics of her own time: Eliza Acton, Dr. Kitchiner, Mrs. Rundell and so on. Typical of an age that had little respect for copyright and a lot of use for plagiarism, Isabella did not give any credit to the authors whose recipes she used so freely but neither did she claim them for her own. The frontispiece of the original edition states quite clearly that the book had been edited, not written, by Mrs. Isabella Beeton, and in all its pages there are only two recipes that she noted as being "the author's own receipts:" the Oxford Sausages and the Soup for Benevolent Purposes. However, she did test them all, altering or amending them where she felt necessary. All the additional information and advice (with the exceptions of the chapters on medicine and law) are also entirely her own, and bear the unmistakable stamp of her practical, organized and down-to-earth character.

It is interesting to speculate what Isabella might have written had she not died of puerperal fever a week after giving birth to her fourth child. That she should have done so does not say much for Victorian postnatal care as she was strong and healthy, and was herself the eldest of seventeen children born to her mother. No doubt much of the confidence that she was to bring to the writing of *The Book of Household Management* sprang from her early years when she had acted *in loco parentis* to all of her own younger brothers and sisters.

Sam Beeton was the son of one of Isabella's mother's old acquaintances from her first marriage when the family had lived in Milk Street in the City of London. The two women remained in touch with each other and in due course Mrs. Dorling's eldest daughter Isabella, who had grown into a "very handsome young woman with heavy brown hair and a great sweetness of expression," met and fell in love with Sam Beeton. The affection was entirely mutual, and after a courtship of a year, which was short by Victorian standards, the couple were married.

Whether or not Isabella was fully aware of what marrying a publisher actually involved when she did so, she accepted her new responsibilities with enthusiasm and Sam rapidly came to rely on her financial judgment as well as her ability to edit and write for his various productions. They started their married life in a substantial villa in Pinner, thirteen miles north of London. There, in 1857, their first son was born, only to die six months later of the croup. In 1862 the lease on the house in Pinner ran out and they moved twenty miles down the Thames to Greenhithe, having spent an uncomfortable six months camping out in Sam's offices in Bouverie Street. This period was made a great deal more harrowing by the death of their second son, who had been born in 1861, from scarlet fever. However, throughout both pregnancies and losses Isabella continued to work on *The Book of Household Management,* Sam's other publications, and then the *Dictionary of Cookery.* In Greenhithe a third son, Orchart, was born in 1863, and the fourth, Mayson, whose birth was to be so soon followed by his mother's death, arrived in 1865.

Isabella's untimely death was followed only a year later by Sam's financial ruin. Ward Lock and Tyler kept him on as editor at a salary of £400 per year. This situation lasted, somewhat uneasily, for eight years, at the end of which, after several court cases, Sam regained the right to publish under his own name but not the control of his previous publications. He might well have rebuilt his business had he not by then been racked with long-standing consumption; it was his health years before that had caused Isabella much disquiet, rather than her own or her children's. Sam died in 1877.

The recipes I have chosen are all from the first edition of *The Book of Household Management,* so are Isabella's own work. In each case the recipes are for six and are simple enough for the least skilled of young cooks. Wherever appropriate I have included Sam's and Isabella's comments and asides on the dishes as these are omitted from most later editions of the book.

WHITE SOUP

Serves 6

Unusually, neither Sam nor Isabella had anything to say about this soup except to note that "a more economical white soup may be made by using common veal stock and thickening with rice, flour and milk." It certainly would have been cheaper (twopence ha'penny per pint as opposed to ninepence) but I suspect not as good.

INGREDIENTS

¾ cup ground almonds
⅔ cup cold cooked veal or chicken
slice of stale white bread
strip of fresh lemon rind
blade of mace, pounded, or ¼ teaspoon
   ground mace
2 quarts good white stock (page 144)
yolks of 2 hard-cooked eggs
1½ cups heavy cream
salt and pepper

Grind or process the almonds, veal or chicken, bread, lemon rind and mace together and put them into a pan. Bring the stock to a boil and pour it over the other ingredients, then bring it all back to a simmer, cover and cook gently for 1 hour. Rub the egg yolks through a strainer into the cream. Add this to the soup, season to taste, bring back to a boil and serve immediately.

SALMON A LA GENEVESE

Serves 6 as a starter, 4 as a main course

"THE MIGRATORY HABITS OF THE SALMON   The instinct with which the salmon revisits his native river is one of the most curious circumstances in its natural history. As the swallow returns annually to its nest, so it returns to the same spot to deposit its ova. This fact would seem to have been repeatedly proved. M. de Lande fastened a copper ring round a salmon's tail, and found that for three successive seasons, it returned to the same place. Dr. Block states that gold and silver rings have been attached by Eastern princes to salmon to prove that a communication existed between the Persian Gulf and the Caspian and Northern seas, and that the experiment succeeded."

INGREDIENTS

1 tablespoon butter
2 shallots, chopped, preferably, or 4
   scallions
2 sprigs of parsley, chopped
2 bay leaves
small bunch of fresh herbs or ½
   teaspoon dried mixed herbs
2 carrots, sliced
generous pinch of mace
generous pinch of black pepper
¼ teaspoon salt
4 tablespoons Madeira or medium
   sherry
1¼ cups white stock (page 144)
2 lb piece of salmon
1 teaspoon all-purpose flour
juice of 1 lemon
1 teaspoon anchovy paste
cayenne
salt
watercress or parsley for garnish

Put half the butter in a heavy pan large enough to hold the piece of salmon and melt slowly. Add the shallots, parsley, bay leaves, herbs, carrots and spices and cook gently for 10 minutes. Add the Madeira or sherry and the stock and simmer for 15 minutes. Lay the salmon on top of the vegetables, cover the pan tightly and cook over a very low heat for 30 minutes, or until the fish is quite cooked. Remove it very carefully from the pan and when it has cooled slightly, skin it. You can also remove the bone but take care not to break up the fillets too much. Lay the fish on a warmed serving dish, cover tightly and keep warm.

Strain the cooking juices and return them to the pan. Add the remaining butter, softened and mixed thoroughly with the flour. Cook for a few minutes until the sauce thickens slightly. Then add the lemon juice, anchovy paste and seasoning to taste. To serve, pour a little of the sauce over the fish and garnish with a little watercress or parsley. Serve the remaining sauce separately.

If you want to make the dish in advance, the salmon can be very successfully reheated, well covered, in a microwave (about 3 minutes on high). If you do not have a microwave, pour a little of the sauce over the fish and heat it, very well covered, in a moderate oven for about 25 minutes. Serve as above.

TO MAKE SAUSAGES – AUTHOR'S OXFORD RECEIPT
Makes about 20 good-sized sausages

"THE LEARNED PIG   That the pig is capable of education, is a fact long known to the world: and though, like the ass, naturally stubborn and obstinate, that he is equally amenable with other animals to caresses and kindness, has been shown from very remote time; the best modern evidence of his docility, however, is the instance of the learned pig, first exhibited about a century since, but which has continued down to our own time by repeated instances of an animal who will put together all the letters or figures that compose the day, month, hour and the date of the exhibition, besides many other unquestioned evidences of memory."

INGREDIENTS

½ lb pork, mixed fat and lean
½ lb lean veal
1 cup ground beef suet
1¾ cups fresh brown bread crumbs
rind of 1 lemon
¼ teaspoon black pepper
¼ teaspoon grated nutmeg
1 heaped teaspoon salt
6 fresh sage leaves or ½ teaspoon dried sage
1 teaspoon dried marjoram
2 tablespoons whole-wheat flour
butter or oil for frying

Note   There is a lot of fat in the sausages so they will soon create plenty of frying fat of their own.

Put all the ingredients except the flour and butter or oil in a food processor, blender or grinder and process or grind finely. Roll the mixture into long sausage shapes or round cakes, coat in the flour and fry gently in the hot butter or oil until the sausages are brown on all sides – about 5 minutes. Serve hot or cold with bread, vegetables or a salad.

TO RAGOUT A DUCK WHOLE
Serves 4 to 6, depending on the size of the duck and how many other courses

"VARIETIES OF DUCK   Naturalists count nearly a hundred different species of ducks and there is no doubt that the intending keeper of these harmless and profitable birds may easily take his choice from amongst twenty different sorts. There is, however, so little difference in the various members of the family, either as regards hardiness, laying, or hatching, that the most incompetent fancier or breeder may indulge his taste without danger of making a bad bargain. In connection with their value for the table, light coloured ducks are always of milder flavour than those that are dark coloured, the white Aylesbury's being general favourites. Ducks reared exclusively on a vegetable diet will have a whiter and more delicate flesh than those allowed to feed on animal offal; while the flesh of birds fattened on the latter food, will be firmer than that of those which have only partaken of food of a vegetable nature."

INGREDIENTS

1 large duck
salt and pepper
2 onions, sliced
6 fresh sage leaves or 1 teaspoon dried sage
3 sprigs of fresh lemon thyme or 1 teaspoon dried lemon thyme
5 cups good beef stock (page 144)
2 tablespoons very soft butter
¼ cup flour, whole-wheat or all-purpose flour
2 cups good quality frozen peas or young fresh peas in season

Season the duck inside and out and prick it thoroughly all over. Roast it, on a rack over a baking pan to allow the fat to run out, at 375° for 20 minutes. Use 2 tablespoons of the duck fat to fry the onions in a pan large enough to hold the duck fairly easily. Remove the duck from the rack and place it on the onions. Add the herbs with the stock, cover, bring to the boil and simmer gently for 1½ hours.

Remove the duck on to a serving dish and keep warm. Skim and remove as much fat as possible

RAGOUT OF WHOLE DUCK (TOP), OXFORD SAUSAGES AND HARICOTS BLANCS A LA MAITRE D'HOTEL

from the stock. Rub the butter into a roux with the flour, and add it to the stock in little knobs. Stir and cook until it thickens slightly, then add the peas. Allow the gravy to return to the boil, adjust the seasoning to taste and serve with the duck.

ROLLED LOIN OF MUTTON
Serves 6

"THE POETS ON SHEEP The keeping of flocks seems to have been the first employment of mankind; and the most ancient sort of poetry was probably pastoral. The poem known as the Pastoral gives a picture of the life of the simple shepherds of the golden age, who are meant to have beguiled their time in singing. In all pastorals, repeated allusions are made to the 'fleecy flocks,' the 'milk white lambs' and 'the tender ewes;' indeed, the sheep occupy a position in these poems inferior only to that of the shepherds who tend them."

INGREDIENTS

about 6 lb loin of mutton (if available;
*   otherwise use mature lamb)*
½ teaspoon pepper
¼ teaspoon ground allspice
¼ teaspoon mace
¼ teaspoon grated nutmeg
6 cloves
2 oz ham or lean bacon
½ cup ground suet
grated rind of 1 lemon
1 teaspoon finely chopped fresh parsley
1 teaspoon mixed fresh sweet herbs
*   (thyme, savory, etc.) or ½ teaspoon*
*   dried mixed herbs*
generous pinch of salt
pinch of cayenne
pinch of mace
2 cups whole-wheat bread crumbs
2 eggs
1 tablespoon whole-wheat or all-
*   purpose flour*
⅔ cup red wine
⅔ cup chicken or beef stock
⅔ cup sliced mushrooms
⅔ cup port
2 tablespoons mushroom catsup

Bone the loin or have it done by the butcher. Mix the pepper, allspice, mace, nutmeg and cloves together and sprinkle over the meat. Leave it for 24 hours.

Make the forcemeat by grinding or processing the ham with the suet, lemon rind, herbs, spices, breadcrumbs and eggs. Spread this mixture over the inside of the loin, roll it up and tie it securely.

Bake on a rack at 350°, allowing 10 minutes per pound. Remove the meat from the oven and allow it to cool.

Remove the fat from the baking dish and, if there are any juices, scrape them into a pan large enough to hold the meat. Sprinkle the meat liberally with the flour and put it in the pan. Add the red wine, stock and mushrooms. Bring to the boil and simmer very gently for a further 10 to 15 minutes per pound, depending on whether you are cooking lamb or mutton.

When the meat is cooked, transfer it from the pan to a warmed serving dish and remove the strings. Add the port and mushroom catsup to the juices in the pan, cook for a further 1 to 2 minutes, adjust the seasoning if necessary and serve with the lamb. Mrs. Beeton suggests you serve it with red currant jelly but I feel this is really *de trop*.

CELERY A LA CREME
Serves 6

"ORIGIN OF CELERY In the marshes and ditches of this country there is to be found a very common plant known by the name of Smallage. This is the wild form of celery; but, by being subjected to cultivation, it loses its acrid nature, and becomes mild and sweet. In its natural state it has a peculiar rank, coarse taste and smell and its root was reckoned by the ancients as one of the 'five greater aperient roots.' There is a variety of this in which the root becomes turnip shaped and large. It is called Celeriae [celeriac] and is extensively used by the Germans, and preferred by them to celery. In a raw state, this plant does not suit weak stomachs; cooked it is less difficult to digestion, although a large quantity should not be taken."

INGREDIENTS

6 medium hearts of celery, well
*   trimmed*
salt
1 cup heavy cream
1 blade of mace, pounded, or ¼
*   teaspoon ground mace*

Slice the celery in two lengthwise. Boil it in plenty of well-salted water until tender – 10 to 15 minutes depending on the size of the heads. Meanwhile, heat the cream with the mace and stir it gently over a low heat for 5 minutes. When the celery is cooked, drain it very thoroughly, lay it in a warmed serving dish and pour over the cream. Serve immediately.

The celery can be reheated, well covered, in a microwave before pouring over the sauce.

STEWED BELGIAN ENDIVE
Serves 6

"This vegetable, so beautiful in appearance, makes an excellent addition to winter salad when lettuces and other salad herbs are not obtainable. It is usually placed in the centre of the dish, and looks remarkably pretty with slices of beetroot, hard-boiled eggs, and curled celery placed around it so that the colours contrast nicely. It may also be served hot, stewed in cream, brown gravy or butter; but when dressed thus, the sauce it is stewed in should not be very highly seasoned, as that would destroy and overpower the flavour of the vegetable. Average cost – 1d per head."

INGREDIENTS

6–9 heads of Belgian endive,
    depending on size
salt
2½ cups white stock (page 144)
1 lump of sugar
2 tablespoons soft butter
¼ cup whole-wheat or all-purpose flour
juice of 1 lemon

Trim the endive thoroughly and blanch it in lightly salted boiling water for 2 minutes. Remove the heads and drain them thoroughly, then slice them thickly. Put the endive in a pan with the white stock, sugar and a little salt. Bring to the boil and simmer for 7 to 10 minutes, or until it is quite tender. Mix the flour thoroughly with the butter and add it to the endive in small knobs. Continue to cook and stir till the sauce thickens slightly. Add the lemon juice, salt and pepper to taste. Transfer to a heated dish and serve.

The endive can be prepared in advance and gently reheated in its sauce on top of the stove.

HARICOTS BLANCS A LA MAITRE D'HOTEL
Serves 6

"HARICOTS AND LENTILLS   Although these vegetables are not much used in this country, yet in France and other Catholic countries, from their peculiar constituent properties, they form an excellent substitute for animal food during Lent and *maigre* days. At the time of the prevalence of the Roman religion in this country, they were probably much more generally used than at present . . . The haulm of the haricot is both of little bulk and little use, but the seed is used in making the esteemed French dish called haricot, with which it were well that the working classes of this country were acquainted. There is, perhaps, no other vegetable dish so cheap and easily cooked, and, at the same time, so agreeable and nourishing . . . From 3,840 parts of a kidney bean Einhoff obtained 1,805 parts of matter analagous to starch, 351 of vegeto-animal matter, and 700 parts of mucilage."

INGREDIENTS

2¼ cups dried navy beans, soaked in
    cold water for 2 hours
¼ cup butter
2 tablespoons very finely chopped
    parsley
salt and pepper
juice of 1–2 lemons

Drain the beans, put into a pan and cover with fresh water. Bring to a boil and simmer gently until they are quite tender – this can take from 45 minutes to 1½ hours depending on the age of the beans. When they are cooked, drain them thoroughly, then mix in the butter, parsley, lemon juice and salt and pepper to taste. Serve hot.

The beans can be prepared in advance and reheated, well covered to prevent them drying out, in a microwave, a moderate oven or, very gently, on top of the stove.

ICED APPLE PUDDING

Serves 6

Like Fannie Farmer thirty years later, Isabella is concerned about the medical effects of ice cream consumption:

"The aged, delicate and children should abstain from ices or iced beverages; even the strong and healthy should partake of them in moderation. They should be taken immediately after the repast, or some hours after, because the taking of these substances *during* the process of digestion is apt to provoke indisposition ... It is also necessary to abstain from them when persons are very warm, or immediately after taking violent exercise, as in some cases they have produced illnesses which have ended fatally."

Not through respect for your health but because the 20th century has a less sweet palate than the 19th, I have reduced the sugar content considerably.

INGREDIENTS

1 lb eating apples, peeled, cored and
    chopped
thinly peeled rind of 1 orange, Seville
    preferably
3 tablespoons apricot jam
2 tablespoons extra-fine sugar
½ cup pitted black cherries, fresh or
    canned
¼ cup raisins, plumped in boiling water
1 tablespoon very finely chopped
    candied peel
¼ cup silvered almonds
¼ cup orange Curaçao
¼ cup Maraschino
1 cup heavy cream

Note Grand Marnier or Cointreau could be substituted for the Curaçao; cherry brandy, Crème de Cassis or Framboise for the Maraschino.

Stew the apples very gently with the orange rind, on top of the stove for about 20 minutes, or in a microwave on medium-high for about 8 minutes. In either case they should be quite soft; take care that they do not burn as no water is added to them. Remove the orange rind and purée the apples with the apricot jam and the sugar. Put the purée into a bowl and leave to cool completely.

Stir the cherries, raisins, peel and almonds into the purée and put the bowl into the freezer to chill thoroughly for about 15 minutes. Whip the cream with the liqueurs until it just holds its shape. Fold it into the apple mixture. Line an ice cream mold if you have one (if not use a jelly mold or ring mold or even a bowl such as you would use for Christmas pudding) with plastic wrap. Pour in the mixture and freeze thoroughly.

To serve, loosen the pudding by wrapping it in a hot cloth, then unmold on to a serving dish. Ideally you should unmold it 15 minutes before you want to serve it and leave it in a refrigerator to soften slightly. Serve with sweet almond or other cookies.

TIPSY CAKE

Serves 6

Isabella (or Sam) appended a long note about almond cultivation to this recipe, but said nothing else about this very popular dish. It was, however, illustrated on a raised cake stand, which is a very effective way of presenting it.

INGREDIENTS

1 stale butter sponge cake, large enough
    to cut into six reasonable portions
6 tablespoons brandy
about 1¼ cups medium sweet sherry or
    sweet white wine
½ cup sliced or slivered almonds
2½ cups rich custard (page 116)

Arrange the portions of cake – a butter sponge is the ideal, fairly solid texture – on a cake stand or serving dish. Prick the sponge all over very thoroughly with a skewer. Mix the brandy with the sherry or wine and pour it slowly over the sponge, allowing it to soak right through – the cake should end up really soggy. Depending on the size of the cake, you may need to use a little more to achieve the desired result. If you like, the almonds can be browned in the oven before sticking them decoratively all over the cake.

Serve accompanied by the custard. Alternatively, you may prefer to serve lightly whipped cream – allow about 1¼ cups.

ICED APPLE PUDDING AND TIPSY CAKE (TOP) WITH WHIPPED CREAM

VICTORIAN KITCHENS AND BATTERIE DE CUISINE

Victorian kitchens were the culmination of a long slow development from the medieval hall with its open fire and its huge spits to Soyer's model kitchen at the Reform Club, Wyattville's lofty chambers at Longleat or the wonderfully preserved kitchen wing at Lanhydrock in Cornwall, six centuries later.

In the country, or in the larger town houses, Victorian kitchens were usually in a separate wing to keep the smell of cooking, and the risk of fire, away from the main house. However, this also meant that hot food sometimes had to travel up to quarter of a mile to the dining room, so seldom reached the table even lukewarm. In smaller houses especially those in the terraces of the cities, kitchens had descended into the basement by the 19th century. As a result they were frequently dank, dark, sooty from the range, and thoroughly unattractive. Small wonder that Victorian ladies preferred to instruct their cooks over breakfast in the dining room and seldom if ever ventured "below stairs." Small wonder also that so many of them had such problems with their staff!

Although it was called a black and evil monster, the arrival of the enclosed range around 1815 radically altered the Victorian kitchen. Dirty, smoky, unreliable and difficult to use as it was, it marked an enormous step forward from the open fire and the enclosed brick hobs that had been the best that had been available before. Previously, all baking had to be done in brick fireplaces built into the chimney piece (if you were lucky

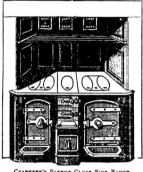

CRABTREE'S PATENT CLOSE FIRE RANGE.
(Another Form.)

enough to have a chimney big, or fire-resistant, enough) or occasionally in little iron ovens under the fire itself. If neither were available, as was the case in many of the smaller and poorer houses, then the food had to be sent to the baker who would rent out his oven space when he had finished his own baking for the day.

Before the introduction of the range, all roasting had to be done in front of open fires, which were immensely hot, extravagant on fuel, relatively inefficient and dangerous. Not only could they all too easily set fire to the whole house, but many hearth deaths were caused by the kitchen women catching their long skirts on the hot coals and incinerating themselves. Small, semi-enclosed "roasters" called Dutch ovens were invented in the 18th century, which maximized the reflected heat from the fire, but they were only practicable for small roasts.

Hob cooking had originally been done over an open fire and although this method was still used in Victorian times, brick hobs with fires below were fairly common from the 16th century onwards. By 1800 iron was used instead of brick and long counters, heated by fires below, could be used for boiling and stewing and for the huge bains-marie, which were used for the more delicate cooking (see the kitchens of the Royal Pavilion at Brighton).

The range combined all these facilities and, by the end of the 19th century, brought them within reach of all but the poorest households. What is more, a range included the extra benefit of a hot

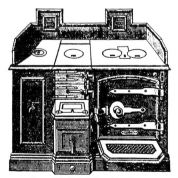

CRABTREE'S PATENT CLOSE FIRE RANGE.

water boiler within its construction, removing yet another hazard (huge pails of boiling water) from the kitchen.

Apart from the range, Victorian kitchens differed little from their earlier counterparts. In a moderate-size house most food would be prepared in the kitchen itself, though there might be a separate larder for storage and maybe the equivalent of a scullery for cleaning game and fish. Larger kitchens were surrounded by a suite of rooms that included preparation kitchens, pastry kitchens, larders, fish and game cleaning and storage areas, pristine dairies, sculleries, pantries and so on. The walls were lined with dressers for the storage of cooking equipment: in the larger houses, ranges of gleaming copper pots, all carefully tinned on the inside to prevent the release of copper acetate when acid foods were cooked; in smaller houses fewer, well used cast-iron pots, kettles and pans.

Bowls for whisking and beating, colanders and sieves, scales, baking tins, preserving pans for the making of jams and jellies, and, in the larger kitchens, innumerable molds of all shapes and sizes for the much loved jellies and creams of the Victorian dessert table, would also be kept on the shelves. By the end of the century, newly invented "gadgets" such as tongue presses, sausage makers, bean slicers, coffee grinders, mincers, can openers and whisks of all shapes and sizes, were also being squeezed on to the shelves.

A large table occupied the center of the kitchen and this was where most of the preparation was done. Basic equipment had changed but little: sharp knives of all sizes, long and short wooden spoons for stirring, ladles for transferring liquids and, most essential, a choice of pestles and mor-

tars. It was not until the invention of the electric food processor in the 20th century that grinding anything from nuts or spices to meat and fish ceased to be a long and laborious task achieved only by constant pounding in the pestle and mortar.

Within such kitchens there might be just the one wretched maid-of-all-work in a poor household, who was expected to cook, clean and serve all on her own, or twenty or thirty staff in the great mansions, ranging from the butler and housekeeper, down through the cook to the kitchen, dairy and scullery maids, each with their own place in the hierarchy and all laboring to serve "the family" above stairs.

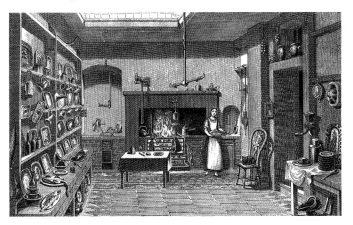

CHAPTER SIX

A BOSTON DINNER
WITH FANNIE FARMER

During the last years of Victoria's reign middle class American women, especially the more intelligent ones who tended to live in and around Boston, were striving for independence – intellectual, financial and political. At the same time scientific and industrial inventions such as calories, light bulbs, telephones and typewriters were rapidly becoming familiar. Why, asked those feminist ladies, could science and industry not be brought to bear on the home, to free the American woman from the age-old drudgery of housekeeping? Surely the wonders of modern science could transform this frequently disorganized, and always monotonous, job into a fulfilling, scientifically based, well-regulated career, guaranteed not only to satisfy the deeper yearnings of the housewife but, also to provide the best environment in which to breed good, strong, worthy American citizens. Central to this transformation, the good ladies believed, was the food on which the "progressive housekeeper" fed her family, thereby molding not only their physical but their moral and intellectual characters.

With the zeal only given to the reformer, and armed with the scientific discoveries of nutritionists such as W. O. Atwater, Professor of Chemistry at Wesleyan University, and a leading light in the "domestic science world," the ladies of the "domestic science movement" set out to reform the American diet along "scientific principles." They analyzed and quantified the nutritive properties of various foods and food combinations. They assessed their digestibility, their different effects on the life styles of their consumers, their ability to promote physical, social, and moral growth and their social acceptability.

OPPOSITE: BOSTON BAKED BEANS (TOP)
AND CONNECTICUT CHOWDER

The only thing that they entirely disregarded, indeed positively disapproved of, was their taste. This oversight was to cause them great problems in the dissemination of their ideas as no matter how willing the great American public was to be convinced of the virtues of food values and scientific eating, they were loathe to abandon all its pleasures in the process.

Nonetheless, by the end of the century "domestic science," under the new name of "home economics," had become an accepted discipline with a place in universities and professional openings in teaching and lecturing. In the 1880s and early 1890s though, the reforming ladies still had to rely on cooking schools to promote their ideas. New York was in fact the first city to establish a cooking school, but the ladies of Boston were not far behind. In 1879 the Women's Education Association decided to follow New York's lead and set up its own Cooking School.

The initial idea of the Boston Cooking School was to instruct, for nominal fees, both women of the lower classes and cooking teachers who would in turn be able to go out and spread the word. The first teachers were a Miss Parloa, who was popular but whose fees grievously stretched the school's budget, and a Joanna Sweeney who had been teaching in the area for some years but who never earned the approval of the organizing committee. The job of running the school finally went to a Mrs. Lincoln who, although she had little experience of either teaching or administration, proved to be a great success, putting together, among other things, the first *Boston Cooking School Cookbook*. Mrs. Lincoln remained in charge of the school until 1885, when she retired to devote herself to "the more lucrative work of writing, editing and lecturing."

Although the school continued to suffer chronic financial problems, it quickly established a formidable reputation and places were eagerly sought by prospective pupils. The students at the main school were predominantly middle class, but very successful evening classes were run for poorer women in the Italian district of the city. The classes at the main school included Plain Cooking, Richer Cooking and Fancy Cooking. But the courses of which its founders and teachers were most proud, and for which the school was most widely respected, were those on invalid cookery (a subject woefully neglected by the medical profession), and the training of the "normal" class whose graduates fanned out to spread the creed of scientific cookery in schools throughout the country.

Fannie Farmer came to this flourishing, if impecunious establishment, relatively late in life. She was born in Boston in 1857, one of four sisters. The brightest of the family, Fannie was destined for college when she contracted what was probably polio. As a result she was bedridden for months, an invalid for several years, could never walk without a limp – and of course lost her chance of going to college. There are many stories of how Fannie became interested first in cooking and then in the Boston Cooking School, but however it happened, in 1888, at the age of thirty-one, she enrolled in the school as a teacher. Mrs. Lincoln had been followed as principal by a series of more or less competent successors. So when the post again fell vacant in 1893, it was offered to Miss Farmer. The Boston School was about to enter its most successful phase.

Although Fannie Farmer believed wholeheartedly in the principles of scientific cooking, she had come to it sufficiently late in life to promote it without dogmatism. Even more important, she loved to eat and saw no reason why her pupils should not enjoy the food that was also good for them. In contrast to the majority of her contemporaries who affected an indifference to food and its taste except in a purely nutritive sense, Fannie describes dishes that were designed to build the moral fiber of the nation as "delicious," "tasty" and "appetizing" – and went out of her way to ensure that they were.

She was a brisk, enthusiastic and "no-nonsense" teacher, a stickler for scientific exactitude (it was she who introduced the "level" teaspoon, tablespoon, etc. into recipes) but with a weakness for inventiveness and garnish that lifted her recipes far above the general run of "scientific" dishes. For example, the menu for the last lecture she gave on dinner party cooking in 1914, only a few weeks before she died, included veal olives with an accompaniment of Thorndyke potatoes – potatoes and bananas mashed together, stuffed into banana skins, sprinkled with Parmesan and browned under the grill. This was followed by a Tango salad – avocados cut to look like horseshoes with bits of truffle representing the nails, the centers filled with orange sections and the whole covered with a cooked dressing of condensed milk, whipped cream and orange juice – and a pineapple bombe "in which pineapple sherbet was used to line a mold that was then filled with custard and candied fruit."

Although the seeds of such frivolity were to be seen in the 1890s when she ran the Boston Cooking School, Fannie's love for creativity and decoration was only really given its head after she left the Boston School to found her own in 1902. But before she did so, she had established an enormous following, drawn, as Laura Shapiro says in her fascinating book *Perfection Salad,* by "her unique combination of directness and novelty."

In 1896 Fannie revised Mrs. Lincoln's original *Boston Cooking School Cookbook*, replacing her predecessor's discursive suggestions with exact instructions and simple scientific explanations. The first book had been continuously in use at the school and had had a limited success outside it. The new edition, which borrowed recipes liberally and, it must be said, without acknowledgment from the original, was printed at Fannie's own expense by a distinguished firm of Boston printers. It had to be reprinted twice in the year it came out, and was reprinted every year until her death in 1915, by which time it had sold over three hundred and sixty thousand copies. Although she was to write five other books between 1898 and 1912, it is with the *Boston Cooking School Cookbook* that she is always associated.

It is from this first edition that I have taken the following recipes, allowing Fannie, wherever possible, to introduce them in her own inimitable style.

CONNECTICUT CHOWDER

Serves 6

"How may a hearty dinner be better begun than with a thin soup? The hot liquid, taken into an empty stomach, acts as a stimulant rather than as a nutrient (as is the popular opinion) and prepares the way for the meal which is to follow. The cream soups and purées are so nutritious that, with bread and butter, they furnish a satisfactory meal." That is certainly true of this Connecticut chowder, which is delicious on a cold winter's night.

INGREDIENTS

1½ lb cod or haddock, with bones if
*   possible*
8 cups water
2½ tablespoons fat salt pork, very
*   finely diced*
1 large onion, finely chopped
1½ lb potatoes, cut in ¾ inch cubes
2 cups very finely chopped tomatoes
2 tablespoons butter
salt and pepper
½ cup graham or other savory crackers,
*   crumbed (optional)*

Remove the bones and skin from the fish, put into a pan with just under half the water, bring to a boil and simmer for 20 minutes. Strain the stock and discard the skin and bones. Cut the fish into 2 inch pieces.

In a largish saucepan, fry the salt pork gently in its own fat for 2 minutes, then add the onion and fry until the onion is soft but not browned. Add the tomatoes, cover and cook gently for a further 10 minutes. Meanwhile, bring the fish stock to a boil, add the potato dice and boil briskly for 5 minutes. Then add, with the remaining water and the fish pieces, to the pork mixture. Bring it all back to a simmer and cook for a further 10 minutes, or until the potatoes and fish are quite cooked. Add the butter and seasoning to taste. Serve in large bowls sprinkled with cracker crumbs.

HAMBURG STEAKS

Serves 6

It always baffled me that a meat patty made exclusively of beef should be called a "ham"burger – until I read Fannie's recipe for Hamburg Steak . . .

INGREDIENTS

2 lb good quality beef (rump, sirloin,
*   etc.)*
1 large onion
3 medium eggs
salt and pepper
nutmeg
butter or oil for frying

Grind the beef with the onion and eggs in a grinder or food processor. Season generously (Fannie says "highly") with salt, pepper and nutmeg. Make the mixture into six large or twelve small patties and fry them reasonably briskly in a little butter or oil for between 2 and 5 minutes, depending on how rare you like your steak.

Fannie says, "serve as Meat Cakes," but gives no further details, so feel free to serve them in a bun or with vegetables such as her Escalloped Cabbage (page 81).

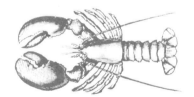

BAKED HALIBUT WITH LOBSTER SAUCE

Serves 6

"Fish meat, with but few exceptions, is less stimulating and nourishing than meat of other animals, but is usually easier of digestion. Salmon, mackerel and eels are exceptions to these rules and should not be eaten by those of weak digestion. White-blooded fish, on account of their easy digestibility, are especially recommended for those of sedentary habits. Fish is not recommended for brain-workers on account of the large amount of phosphorus (an element abounding largely in nerve tissue) which it contains, but because of its easy digestibility."

INGREDIENTS

2½ lb piece of halibut
about 2 oz fatty salt pork, cut in very
*   thin 1 inch long slivers*
salt and pepper
whole-wheat flour
2 tablespoons butter
2½ cups water
1 large sprig of parsley
2 bay leaves
3 slices of onions
3 slices of carrot

Lay the halibut in a baking pan. Cut small, deep slashes in its flesh and insert the slivers of pork. Sprinkle the halibut quite generously with salt, pepper and whole-wheat flour and dot it with the butter. Pour the water round the fish, then add the parsley and bay leaves, roughly broken up, with the slices of onion and carrot.

Cover the pan tightly with foil and bake at 350° for 40 minutes. Remove on to a warmed dish and serve accompanied by the lobster sauce (right).

LOBSTER SAUCE

In Fannie's day, along the Massachusetts coast, lobsters would have been quite cheap enough to use for a sauce. Unless you are feeling like splashing out, you may prefer to use a less expensive shellfish such as crayfish or large shrimps.

INGREDIENTS

about ¾ lb uncooked lobster tails, or
*   other shellfish, in their shells*
5 cups boiling water
4 tablespoons butter
5 tablespoons all-purpose flour
salt and cayenne
juice of 1 lemon
⅔ cup heavy cream (optional)

Put the shellfish into a pan and pour on the boiling water. Cook briskly for 4 to 7 minutes depending on the type of shellfish, then remove them from the pan with a perforated spoon and leave to cool slightly. As soon as you can handle them, remove the flesh from the shells and return the latter to the water. Continue to boil briskly, uncovered, till the liquid is reduced to 3 cups, then strain it.

Melt the butter in a separate pan, add the flour and cook together for a few minutes. Add the strained stock slowly and cook and stir until the sauce thickens. Chop the shellfish into smallish pieces and add to the sauce. Season to taste with salt, cayenne and the lemon juice. Fannie served her sauce with no further additions, but for a richer texture, add the cream and adjust the seasoning once again. Serve with the baked halibut (left).

OPPOSITE: BAKED HALIBUT WITH LOBSTER SAUCE, HAMBURG STEAKS (TOP) AND ESCALLOPED CABBAGE

VEAL BIRDS

Serves 6

Fannie is not very enthusiastic about veal – "being deficient in fat and having but little flavor, pork or butter should be added while cooking [veal], and more seasoning is required than for cooking other meats" – yet she still gives ten recipes for veal dishes. She only gives twenty for beef, which she describes as "the most nutritious and largely consumed of all animal foods." The veal "birds" are excellent but can just as successfully be made with pork tenderloin, which cuts down their cost substantially.

INGREDIENTS

2 lb escalope of veal or pork tenderloin opened out into one piece
¼ lb fatty salt pork in one piece
¼ cup graham or other savory cracker crumbs
1 egg
juice of 1 small onion
juice of ½ lemon
salt and black pepper
cayenne
2⅓ tablespoons butter
2 tablespoons seasoned all-purpose flour
1¼ cups heavy cream

Get the butcher to pound the escalopes or pork tenderloin reasonably flat. Cut the meat into twelve rectangles, about 4×2 inches in size, and save any trimmings. Put each rectangle of meat between two pieces of wax paper and beat them as thin as you can with a mallet, rolling pin or the flat side of a cleaver.

Chop the veal or pork trimmings and the salt pork very finely (you could use a food processor but the texture will be slightly different) and put them into a bowl. Add the cracker crumbs, egg, onion juice (it can be squeezed through a garlic press) and lemon juice. Season generously with salt, pepper and cayenne and mix the stuffing together well.

Divide the stuffing into twelve portions and lay one down the middle of each rectangle of meat. Fold the meat over and attach it to itself with a toothpick. Melt the butter in a heavy flat pan. Roll the "birds" in the seasoned flour, then fry them briskly in the butter until they are well browned on all sides. Add the cream, reduce the

heat, cover the pan and simmer gently for 20 minutes. Adjust the seasoning of the sauce to taste and thin it slightly with a little white wine or water if necessary before serving. Rice or creamed potatoes and a green vegetable such as lightly boiled spinach are best with the "birds."

BOSTON BAKED BEANS

Serves 6

"The fine reputation which Boston Baked Beans have gained has been attributed to the earthen bean-pot with small top and bulging sides in which they are supposed to be cooked. Equally good beans have often been eaten where a five pound lard pail was substituted for the broken bean pot."

INGREDIENTS

3½ cups navy beans, soaked in cold water overnight
1 lb piece fatty salt pork with the rind left on
1 heaped teaspoon salt
2 tablespoons molasses
2 heaped tablespoons raw cane sugar
1 tablespoon wholegrain mustard
2½ cups boiling water

Note Fannie says that the mustard helps to digest the beans.

Drain the beans, put into a pan and cover with fresh water. Heat very gently and cook at just below boiling point for 30 minutes. Scald the pork in boiling water for 2 minutes and if necessary scrape the rind clean with the back of a knife; cut a thin slice off the pork and lay it in the bottom of a bulging-sided bean pot if you have one, if not an ovenproof casserole or a slow cookpot. Drain the beans and pour them into the pot over the pork. Cut through the rind of the remaining pork every 1 inch or so and bury it in the beans, leaving the rind exposed. Mix the salt, molasses, sugar and mustard in a bowl and add the boiling water; mix well and pour over the beans. Add more water until the beans are just covered.

Cover the pot and cook very slowly – either for 6 to 8 hours at 225° or overnight in a slow cookpot. Uncover the pot for the last hour to allow the pork rind to crisp up before serving. If you are using a slow cookpot, transfer the mixture to an ordinary pot to complete the cooking. Like all bean pots, the taste of the beans will improve if kept for a day or two.

ESCALLOPED CABBAGE
Serves 6

Fannie starts her chapter on vegetables by quoting Professor Atwater's table breaking down the composition of the commonest vegetables into their proteid, fat, carbohydrate, mineral matter and water parts. Cabbage is 2.1% proteid, 0.4% fat, 5.8% carbohydrate, 1.4% mineral and 90.3% water; compared to most other vegetables, it comes out well in the mineral ratings. This would make it popular with Fannie as she points out that most vegetables "are chiefly valuable for their potash salts, and should form part of each day's dietary."

INGREDIENTS

6 cups fairly thinly sliced fresh green
* cabbage*
5 heaped tablespoons butter
3 tablespoons flour, all-purpose or
* whole-wheat*
2 cups milk
salt and pepper
⅔ cup graham or other savory cracker
* crumbs*

Cook the cabbage in 2 inches fast-boiling water for about 10 minutes, or until it is cooked but still slightly crunchy. Meanwhile, melt 3 tablespoons of the butter in a pan, add the flour and cook together for a couple of minutes. Add the milk gradually, stirring continuously to prevent the sauce becoming lumpy. Season to taste with salt and pepper.

Drain the cabbage well, then mix the sauce into it thoroughly. Spoon into an ovenproof pie dish or casserole. Melt the remaining butter and mix it with the crumbs. Spread this topping over the cabbage and bake, uncovered, at 350° for 30 minutes.

CORN OYSTERS
Serves 6

In Professor Atwater's table corn has 2.8% proteid (moderately high), 1.1% fat, 14.1% carbohydrate, 0.7% mineral matter and 81.3% water. Although nowhere near the league of lima beans (7.1% proteid) or green peas (4.4%) their proteid level would still allow them, in Fannie's estimation, "to be used in place of flesh foods."

INGREDIENTS

6 ears of corn or 1½ cups frozen or
* canned corn*
2 medium eggs
⅓ cup whole-wheat flour
4 tablespoons sunflower or corn oil for
* frying*

Grate the corn into a bowl or, if you are using the frozen or canned corn, process or chop roughly in a blender. Whip the eggs, then beat in the flour and mix into the grated or processed corn. Form the mixture into six large or twelve small pancakes. Heat the oil in a large flat pan and fry the pancakes briskly for 2 to 3 minutes on each side. Drain on paper towels and serve hot.

STEAMED BLUEBERRY PUDDING WITH CREAMY SAUCE

Serves 6

Unusually, Fannie gives no introduction at all to her chapters on Hot Puddings, Pudding Sauces or Cold Desserts – maybe feeling that there was too little "nourishment" in them to justify a scientific preamble.

INGREDIENTS

2½ cups all-purpose or whole-wheat
flour
4 teaspoons baking powder
generous pinch of salt
5 tablespoons butter
1 cup milk
1 cup blueberries, or other berries

Sift the dry ingredients together. Work in 4 tablespoons of the butter with the tips of the fingers. Add the milk and the berries and mix to a soft dough. Grease a 1-quart bowl with the re-maining butter and pour in the dough. Cover tightly and steam for 1½ hours. You could also cook the pudding in a microwave on high for 8 minutes, then allow it to stand for 5, although the texture will not be quite so good. Unmold the pudding on to a warm plate and serve with Creamy Sauce (below).

CREAMY SAUCE

Fannie does not include any cornstarch in this sauce and warns of the danger of curdling. I thought it safer to include a small amount of cornstarch which does not affect the taste but does prevent curdling.

INGREDIENTS

1 stick butter
⅔ cup confectioners' sugar
1 tablespoons cornstarch
½ cup white wine
½ cup milk

Cream the butter in a small pan with the sugar and the cornstarch. When they are absolutely smooth, put the pan over a low heat and stir in the wine and the milk very gradually. Cook until the sauce is smooth and creamy, without letting it boil, then serve with steamed pudding. As long as you use the cornstarch, the sauce can be made in advance and reheated gently before serving.

CANTON SHERBET

Serves 6

"Ices and other frozen dishes comprise the most popular desserts. Hygienically speaking, they cannot be recommended for the final course of a dinner, as cold mixtures reduce the temperature of the stomach, thus retarding digestion until the normal temperature is again reached. But how cooling, refreshing, and nourishing, when pro-perly taken, and of what inestimable value in the sick room!" What more can one say?

INGREDIENTS

2 oz stem ginger
2 cups water
¼ cup extra-fine sugar
½ cup fresh orange juice
juice of 1 medium lemon

Note Fannie used twice the amount of sugar but I found it a good deal too sweet.

Cut the ginger into small pieces and add it to the water and sugar in a pan. Bring to a boil and sim-mer for 15 minutes. Add the fruit juices, cool and strain. Freeze in an ice cream maker if you have one. If not, freeze the sherbet in a bowl but make sure that you take it out of the freezer and beat it thoroughly every 10 to 15 minutes until it is frozen to prevent large ice crystals forming.

OPPOSITE: STEAMED BLUEBERRY PUDDING WITH CREAMY SAUCE (BELOW) AND CANTON SHERBET

BEVERAGES

Much to the disturbance of the growing temperance movement, the drinking of alcohol was a pastime enjoyed by the majority of Victorian Englishmen – whether it was consumed in the lowest beer shop or at an aristocratic dinner table. "Soft" drinks were, of course, also readily available.

The street stalls to be found in most cities sold ginger beer, lemonade, hot and cold cordials or sweet fruit syrups and "peppermint water," as well as prodigious quantities of coffee, cocoa and, particularly, tea. Until the beginning of the 19th century, tea had been imported solely – and at considerable cost – from China. It had therefore remained a somewhat exclusive drink. However, the growth of tea estates in India and the expansion of the East India Company meant that the new varieties of Indian tea were soon available in abundance – and their prices tumbled. As a result, hot, sweet tea – often, since tea merchants were no more honest than others, made from heavily adulterated leaves – became the standard drink of the very poor. It was cheap and gave a feeling of warmth and instant energy although its actual nutritional content was nonexistent.

Milk was drunk regularly where it was available: on the larger farms and country estates; in the city parks where herds of cows continued to graze until the 20th century; and from the city dairies, although the cows were normally kept in such appalling conditions that their milk was often thin and sour.

Water was also much drunk although its quality varied from pure spring to foul and polluted in some of the worst slum areas of the big cities. Spa waters were popular with all classes: poor Londoners would have a day out at Hampstead or Islington to "take the waters," while their more prosperous neighbors might venture to Harrogate, Bath, Cheltenham or Tunbridge Wells. Bottled spring waters, such as Malvern, and aerated distilled waters were also favored – indeed, the noted Victorian author, Sir Henry Thompson suggests that "those who drink water with their meal probably enjoy the pleasure of eating more than those who drink wine – they certainly preserve an appreciative palate longer than the wine drinker."

Beer remained a popular drink among the working and lower middle classes, although it was seldom found in the households of those who aspired to elevate themselves in the world. During the 18th century the sale of beer had been restricted to the large brewers who alone were licensed to run public houses. However, the bitterly contested Beer Act in 1830 removed almost all restrictions from those wishing to sell beer. As a result, beer shops mushroomed throughout the early years of Victoria's reign. Most of these were in run-down areas and catered for the very poor who had been unable to afford the higher prices charged in the licensed public houses. The larger brewers also benefited from the lifting of restrictions; over the next fifty years, they invested heavily in large, solid, plush and comfortable public houses (many of which are still to be found in the older towns and cities) to attract the growing numbers of the lower middle classes and the better paid working men.

But it was wine that was the drink of the dinner table. Not English-grown wine (the few, even partially successful attempts at commercial vineyards, such as Lord Bute's at Castle Coch, were laughed to shame in "good society") but

the wines of France, Spain and Portugal. Sir Henry Thompson, in his immensely popular *Food and Feeding* (it had reached its eleventh edition by 1901) discusses the question of "wine with dinner" at some length.

He prefaces his advice with the observation that the consumption of alcoholic drinks "is a physiological error for, say, nineteen persons out of twenty," but excuses his own indulgence on the grounds that "no particular harm can result from the habit of now and then enjoying a glass of really fine pure wine – and, rare as this is, I do not think any other is worth consuming." However, this nectar should "never be taken, in any form or under any circumstances, before dinner, that is, on an empty stomach, and also is not desirable after the meal is finished. Regarded from a gastronomic point of view alone, nothing should appear afterwards except a small glass of cognac and coffee." Sir Henry is equally firm in banishing the "spirituous aperitifs" that were growing in popularity as pre-prandial drinks, and the "sweet compounds and fruity juices which not very long ago were produced, and in-

ordinately puffed, in lieu of wines as dinner drinks."

Having insisted that the quality of the wines should only be of the best, he suggests the following selection to accompany a moderately luxurious dinner – then goes on to warn that a mixture of red and white wine, and an over-indulgence in Champagne, "however delightful each may prove itself in passing over the palate, often quarrel sadly when they arrive in the stomach below . . .

"Briefly, the rule is to offer a glass of light pale sherry or a dry Sauternes after the soup; a delicate Rhine wine or Moselle after fish; a glass of good Bordeaux with the joint of mutton; the same, or champagne – dry, but with some true vinous character in it – during the entrées; the best red wine in the cellar, Bordeaux or Burgundy, with the grouse or other roast game. With the ice or dessert, a glass of full flavoured but matured champagne, or a liqueur may be served."

Despite Sir Henry's protestations, the consumption of alcohol "in society" was obviously just as high as among the lower orders. However, by the time that he was writing in the 1880s and 1890s, the Temperance movement had made some progress among all ranks of society. Not only were the working classes being drawn from the pubs and the beer houses to the working mens' clubs, the coffee and tea houses, the choral societies and the football clubs, but upper class dinner parties no longer conformed to the pattern described by the socialite, Captain Gronow in the early years of Victoria's reign:

"Most men and many women drink heavily as soon as they have tasted their soup; as from that moment everyone is taking wine with everybody else till the close of dinner. After the ladies have departed, the gentlemen settle down to consume one or two bottles of port each – as a result of which female society, among the upper classes, is most notoriously neglected – except by romantic foreigners . . ."

A DINNER AT MR. KETTNER'S SOHO RESTAURANT

K ettner's *Book of the Table* first appeared, anonymously, in 1877 and was assumed, reasonably enough, to have been written by the owner of the by then very successful Soho restaurant. In fact, the book was written by the distinguished journalist, E. S. Dallas, a frequent, if anonymous, contributor to *The Times* of London and a much respected theatrical and literary critic of the 1850s and 1860s. Kettner's name was given to it because, as Dallas explained in a letter to a colleague in 1878 (quoted in Derek Hudson's 1968 edition of the book), "he has undertaken the responsibility of the practical receipts – a point of some importance as affecting the sale of the work." In fact the "receipts" form a quite small part of the book; the vast majority of it is made up of amusing, witty, scholarly and fascinating articles on every aspect of food and eating, laid out in the form of an encyclopedia.

E. S. Dallas was born in 1828 in Jamaica, of Scottish parentage. He was brought to England at an early age and sent, eventually, to Edinburgh where he studied philosophy and wrote for the *Edinburgh Guardian*. The collapse of the newspaper, and his marriage to Isabella Glynn, a successful Shakespearean actress, persuaded him to move to London where he started to write for *The Times*. Over the next twenty years Dallas was to write continuously and successfully – although anonymously as was the fashion – for the paper; he was "a gentleman of great attainments and erudition, much distinguished as the writer of the best critical literary pieces in *The*

Times" according to Charles Dickens, and "a Prince among journalists" according to his equally successful colleague, George Augustus Sala.

By the 1870s though Dallas had fallen on hard times. He had ceased to write regularly for the *Times*, his marriage had broken up, and his book, *The Gay Science*, which "attempted to settle the first principles of Criticism, and to show how alone it can be raised to the dignity of a science" had attracted much critical acclaim but few readers. He was in financial difficulties and his health was failing.

He had long been friendly with Auguste Kettner, Napoleon III's erstwhile chef, who had opened a restaurant at 29 Romilly Street, Soho in 1867. At that time Soho was known as the seedy abode of foreigners and not at all the sort of place where one would wish to dine. However, an "anonymous" but very appreciative account in *The Times* in 1869 of a dinner eaten at Kettner's restaurant, "which was better than could have been obtained at a West End club and which cost considerably less" did much to change this impression. Two years later Kettner's was mentioned in a guidebook for American visitors to London and by 1880 the restaurant, then run by Kettner's son-in-law, had expanded to fill four houses in Romilly Street. The *cabinets particuliers*, or private dining rooms, which still exist, were particularly popular with diners wishing for a quiet tête à tête.

The Kettners did not forget the "anonymous" author of their first favorable review and it is likely that they did much to support the journalist while he was working on *The Book of the Table*. In fact Dallas survived the book's publication by only two years, dying at the early age of fifty-one in 1879. But "neither ill health nor evil circumstances had abated by one jot the vigour of his intellect nor his sweet disposition and charming ways." *The Book of the Table* is witty, erudite, idiosyncratic, immensely informative, filled with common sense and a true appreciation of good food. I have allowed Dallas to introduce each of the dishes for which I have included a recipe, but to give a fuller flavor of the man and the book here are a few other extracts:

"It is always assumed that a cookery book will make a good cook. Nothing can be more false. If a man or a woman has not the soul of a cook, the most minute receipts will only end in failure. If on the other hand the soul of a cook is there, it is almost always enough to give general rules and leading principles and leave the cook to make variations according to his taste or means. Lord Byron in Italy, gave the most minute directions for his plum pudding; it came out like a broth and was served in a tureen. The great thing it cannot be too often repeated, is to teach a principle and then its application to special cases will follow as a matter of course . . ."

"ARTICHOKE   It is good for a man to eat thistles, and to remember that he is an ass. But an artichoke is the best of thistles, and the man who enjoys it has the satisfaction of feeling that he is an ass of taste. There are several elaborate ways of dressing the artichoke – the Barigoule way and the Lyonnese for example, which have little to recommend them but their elaboration. Each is a mountain of labour for a mouse of result. The result is not bad; but it is always melancholy to see waste – and in art especially the pleasure of it is destroyed where we are made conscious of effort. The Barigoule and Lyonnese receipts are frantic attempts to paint the lily and perfume the violet. When a great cook brings the whole battery of his kitchen to bear upon a simple artichoke bottom, one is reminded of Victor Hugo's comparison: 'It is as if the Deity were to bombard a lettuce with a thunderbolt.' Depend upon it, the simplest way of dressing the artichoke is the best."

"BAIN MARIE (Mary's bath)   This Mary was a Jewess who lived in the fourth century of our era, and was devoted to alchemy. She required a bath that would retain heat long at an equable temperature for the metals and vessels upon which she made her experiments. To this end she heated sand and plunged her vessels into it. The modern Mary bath is an imitation in hot water, which is not so good as sand since it has no special aptitude for retaining the heat, but has the advantage of being easily kept hot by connection with the boiler . . ."

"BREAD   The English bread, as a rule, is so bad at our dinner tables that it has been displaced by the potato. The Englishman wants a potato with every dish that comes before him; the Frenchman on the other hand eats bread throughout the dinner. The bread or potato thus eaten throughout a meal serves two ends; it supplies the farinaceous element of the food and it acts upon the palate as a sponge to prepare it for a new experience. Which for the latter purpose is more serviceable – the bread or the potato? Suppose one were tasting wine: will the French wine taster ever come to eating potatoes between his sips of different vintages? He eats bread which is the best thing possible for the renovation of his taste. Here is a marked point in which the French are ahead of the English in understanding the laws of gustation. They leave the potato to the Englishmen; they choose bread for themselves, and take care to have bread of the best."

"CLEANLINESS   There are few satires on modern civilisation which bite deeper than the incessant inculcation of cleanliness in cookery books. It appears not to be enough to insist in general terms on this virtue, and to take for granted that it will be observed. Indeed it would be possible to quote hundreds of receipts in which the writers cannot mention a single utensil of the kitchen without on each occasion stipulating in an adjective that it shall be clean. What a satire on our way of living if these reiterated injunctions are really needed!"

"EPIGRAM   'I have been dining,' said a French nobleman to one of those wealthy but often ignorant tax farmers who used to be called financiers in France – 'I have been dining with a poet who regaled us at dessert with a choice epigram.' The financier went home to his cook and asked him: 'How comes it that you never send any epigrams to my table?' The next day the cook sent to his table an Epigram of Lamb . . ."

"PUREE   One of the leading points of difference between English and French cookery turns on the greater carefulness of the latter in making a Purée. It is not a question of skill; it is wholly one of good faith. The English cook is content with slovenly work; hence mashed potatoes full of lumps and spinach full of strings and coarse. The English cook shirks the labour of the sieve. If the thing is worth doing it is worth doing well . . . the result depends not upon skill but upon honesty. It is the honesty of their work, as much as anything else, that gives the French cooks their superiority in dressed vegetables."

"SPRATS and their euthanasia. The following receipt for turning sprats into roses – the sublime of cookery – is borrowed from a private letter: 'Some time since C. went to visit a friend in the country who had the most marvellous roses in full bloom. Everyone exclaimed at their beauty and asked "How can you get such?" The gentleman who owned them was a man of few words, and only said, "Sprats." It seemed that he manured them with loads of stinking sprats. Not long afterwards a man called at my house with sprats. "Are they stinking?" said I, eagerly. "No," said the man, "quite fresh." "Then bring me the first stinking ones you have." In a few days he came with a heavy heart, and offered me a large quantity which had turned putrid on his hands. The result was that on a very small bush I had thirty-six blossoms all at once of magnificent Marshal Niels.'"

SKATE BAKED WITH GRUYERE

Serves 6

"To do him honour at table, there should be music with the skate, for he loves it. One way of catching him used to be by playing the fiddle. His love of melody was such that he came to the boat and was ensnared . . . He ought always to be served with his liver, which, if this organ be the seat of the affections in fish, cannot but be good in the skate – the most affectionate fish in the world, a good father, a good mother and fond of family life. He is generally sold at the fishmonger's crimped – that is, cut in strips and rolled around. He is eaten in England plain boiled, with ordinary butter sauce to which mustard is sometimes added, or else capers, but for triumphant occasions take the following receipt."

INGREDIENTS

2 lb boneless skate (you will need a fish weighing about 4½ lb)
6–8 tablespoons butter
2½ cups milk
2 heaped teaspoons cornstarch
4 cloves
2 bouquets garnis
salt and pepper
4 shallots, preferably, or 4 pearl onions, finely chopped
12 very small onions, peeled and kept whole, or 6 larger ones, halved or quartered
1½ cups grated Gruyère cheese
6 thin slices of whole-wheat bread

Cut the skate in thick strips and roll them up. Put the fish in a wide pan with 2 tablespoons of the butter, the milk mixed with the cornstarch, the cloves, bouquets garnis, salt, pepper and chopped shallots or onions. Cover the pan, bring to the boil and simmer for 10 minutes. Meanwhile, spread half the grated cheese over the bottom of a flattish ovenproof dish. Cook the very small onions in a little boiling water for about 10 minutes or until they are tender, then drain them. Fry the slices of bread in the remaining butter until brown and crisp, then cut each piece into four triangles.

Arrange the fried bread around the outside of a serving dish. With a perforated spoon lift the rolls of fish from the poaching liquid and lay them over the cheese, interspersed with the onions. Strain the poaching liquid over the fish and sprinkle the remaining cheese on top. Bake the dish at 350° for 20 minutes to warm it through and brown the top before serving. The Victorians would no doubt have eaten their skate with plain boiled potatoes, but I think the addition of a green vegetable would be an improvement.

CHICKEN A LA MARENGO
Serves 6

"*Chicken à la Marengo* . . . the warrior's chicken . . . betrays hastiness of preparation, and turns the fault into a victory. It is fried in oil, and this oil is afterwards worked into the sauce. But whereas all other sauces must be carefully freed from the appearance of oils and fats which have not incorporated with them – and this is often a tedious process – the chicken of the battle is sent to the table with the superfluous oil floating loose about the dish . . . Its admirers declare that the battle of Marengo was well fought as a preliminary to the chicken of the name."

INGREDIENTS

*½ cup good olive oil, well seasoned
    with salt and black pepper
1 large chicken, divided into six pieces
2 garlic cloves, crushed
6 shallots, preferably, or 3 small onions,
    finely chopped
2 bouquets garnis
2 tablespoons tomato paste
¾ cup good brown sauce (page 145)
generous pinch of sugar
juice of ½–1 lemon*

Heat the seasoned oil in a wide pan and fry the chicken pieces briskly for 20 minutes, turning them so that they get well browned but not burned on all sides. Add the garlic, shallots or onions and bouquets garnis, cover the pan and cook more gently for a further 10 minutes. Remove the chicken pieces to a heated serving dish and keep them warm. Add the tomato paste and brown sauce to the oily juices in the pan and stir well together, then strain the mixture into a clean pan. Add the sugar, further seasoning and lemon juice to taste and pour the sauce over the chicken before serving with boiled potatoes.

Dallas and Kettner suggest garnishing the dish with "fried bread and eggs fried in oil," but I feel that this might be a little too much for 20th century tastes.

CARBONADED SHOULDER OF LAMB OR MUTTON WITH SOUBISE SAUCE
Serves 6

Mutton was far easier to obtain than lamb in Victorian times and its stronger flavor was greatly appreciated. Today mutton is hard to find in ordinary butchers, but end-of-season lamb will make an acceptable substitute. Dallas' remarks on carving a shoulder will be an education to many a 20th century host:

"Shoulder of mutton is a joint about which there would be less controversy if people knew how to carve it. . . . In nine cases out of ten, when mine host carves this joint he helps himself from the bend of the joint, where he can cut the easiest, and sends away the bladebone, where the most perfect morsels lie. Many cookery books give elaborate directions how to carve; but not one points out that the best of the shoulder of mutton is to be found on the upper surface of the bladebone, against the ridge, and after that the under part of the blade is richest in dainty morsels. The shoulder of mutton is usually roasted, but being flat and comparatively thin is easily grilled; and a carbonade of its blade (slashed and scored to increase the broiling surface and permit the penetration of pepper and salt) has for centuries been a celebrated dish. The favourite garniture for a shoulder of mutton has long been stewed onions – whole, sliced or mashed. For whole onions choose the Spanish; for a mash take the Soubise or Breton receipt."

"*Carbonade* If cookery is ever to be an exact science it must be exact in its nomenclature . . . The carbonade has degenerated in France into a stew, having originally meant a grill; and attempts are made to introduce the word into England as corrupted by the French . . . But to do justice to French cooks, the carbonade of mutton with them has come to be a stew because it was thought good to parboil the shoulder before sending it to the grill."

INGREDIENTS

1 large shoulder of end-of-season lamb
*   or a small shoulder of mutton*
2 bouquets garnis
1 teaspoon sea salt
1 teaspoon black peppercorns
4–6 heaped teaspoons made English
*   mustard*
12–15 grinds of black pepper
2–3 heaped teaspoons fine sea salt

Put the shoulder into a large pan with the bouquets garnis, sea salt and black pepper and cover with water. Bring to a boil and simmer, allowing 12 minutes per pound, skimming off any scum

CARBONADED SHOULDER OF LAMB WITH SOUBISE SAUCE

that may rise to the surface. Remove the meat from the water (which can be used to make soup), drain and dry it. Blade side upwards, score the meat deeply every 1½ inches. Mix the mustard (how much you use will depend on how fiery you want your carbonade to be) with the salt and pepper and rub it well into the meat and down the slashes. Cook under a moderately hot broiler for a further 8 minutes per pound, taking care that the meat does not get so close to the heat as to burn. Serve with stewed onions or a Soubise sauce (overleaf).

SOUBISE SAUCE

INGREDIENTS

4 medium onions, finely ground in a
*   food processor if possible*
1¼ cups chicken or veal stock
2 teaspoons cornstarch
1¼ cups heavy cream
pinch of sugar
salt and pepper

Put the onions into a pan with the stock, bring to a boil and simmer for 20 minutes. Add the cornstarch, then stir in the cream, bring back to a boil and cook for a further few minutes. Purée the mixture in a food processor or blender, then rub it through a strainer into a clean pan. Add sugar, salt and pepper to taste and reheat gently before serving.

LIVER AND BACON
Serves 6

"LIVER   Tell it not in Gath – but it is notorious that there are three dishes which, if put upon the bill of fare in a club, are devoured before all else; so that at seven or eight o'clock, when most members dine, there is nothing of them but the tempting words on the dinner-bill. These dishes are Irish stew, tripe and onions, liver and bacon. What a tribute this to the homely cookery of England!"

Homely the dish may be, but cheap it certainly is not. However, do not be tempted to use any liver but calf's if you wish to achieve the proper – and delectable – effect.

INGREDIENTS

olive oil
12 slices of fatty bacon
6 slices of calf's liver
2 teaspoons whole-wheat flour
6 tablespoons meat juices, gravy or
*   good brown sauce (page 145)*
2 tablespoons walnut pickle liquor
*   (optional)*
juice of ½–1 lemon (optional)

Smear olive oil over the base of a wide, heavy pan. Fry the bacon briskly until it is crisp and brown – it needs to be crisp to contrast with the unctuousness of the liver. Remove the bacon to a heated serving dish, reduce the heat slightly and fry the liver slices for 2 minutes on each side, or until they are well browned on the outside but still pink in the middle. Remove them to the serving dish – Dallas says they should be "dished in alternate order with the rashers of bacon." Add the flour, stir well for a few minutes for the flour to cook, then add the meat juices, gravy or sauce. Stir again and cook until the sauce thickens – you may then need to thin it with a little water. At this point it can be seasoned and served spooned over the liver and bacon. Dallas suggests that "some people like a little acid in the sauce," and certainly I found that the pickle liquor and lemon juice tempered its richness admirably.

ROAST VEAL A LA CREME
Serves 8

"When Dr. Lister, who was one of Queen Anne's physicians, went to Paris at the beginning of the last century, he declared that the French might have beef and mutton equal to ours – but we have by far the best veal in Europe. The judgement must now be reversed . . . This is not the fault of the calf, but of the butcher who bleeds the animal a little at a time for days before it is slaughtered. The result is that the veal comes to the table very white, but is often tasteless and stringy. . . . the treatment of veal is not understood in England, and it is only in England that people have turned it into a byword. Macaulay hated Croker with a mortal hatred. His detestation expressed itself in the phrase – 'I hate him worse than cold boiled veal.' There is another well known saying, but it is not his – that to eat veal is as insipid as kissing one's sister."

The quality of veal in the 1980s is usually high, but so is the price. Despite his lack of enthusiasm for veal Dallas gives no less than sixteen recipes for it, the most delicious being the following.

INGREDIENTS

about 5 lb loin of veal
flour
2½ cups heavy cream
½ lb button mushrooms, wiped and halved
⅔ cup dry white wine
salt and pepper

Cover the veal with a piece of buttered foil and roast at 350°, allowing 30 minutes per pound. Twenty minutes before it is done, remove the foil, dust the meat lightly with flour and pour over the cream. Baste with the cream and pan juices occasionally until the meat is cooked. Meanwhile, stew the mushrooms in the wine for 2 minutes. When the meat is cooked, remove it to a warmed serving dish, put the roasting pan over a low heat and add the mushrooms. Stir the mixture thoroughly making sure that you incorporate any burned bits off the bottom of the pan. Adjust the seasoning to taste, and thin the sauce, if necessary, with a little boiling water. Serve the veal immediately, accompanied by the sauce.

BEEFSTEAK WITH OYSTER SAUCE

Serves 6

"BEEF   The influence of the ox on human society, and more especially on the temperament of Mr. John Bull, deserves a chapter to itself. There is room for but a word. No animal has so often been taken for a god as the bull, or for a goddess as the cow; and though we may not be able to allow them so much honour, it cannot be denied that those races of men who own the best of them and partake the most of them have attained the highest civilisation ... Beefsteak is even more popular in England than roast beef and the favourite in this country appears to be a rump-steak. Needless to say that the steak which has attained pre-eminence is always grilled, is served as hot as possible, with the taste of fire on it, and is eaten for the most part plain, in the juice that oozes from it, or with a pat of fresh butter upon it. When an Englishman does take a sauce with his steak, oyster sauce is what he first thinks of."

INGREDIENTS

6 good rump steaks
6 large or 12 small fresh oysters with their juices
4 tablespoons very soft butter
¼ cup all-purpose flour
salt and pepper
nutmeg
about 1 cup milk

Cook the steaks under a very hot broiler for 2 to 8 minutes each side, depending on how rare you like them. Meanwhile, cook the oysters very gently in their own juice (if you boil them quickly they will be tough) for 5 minutes. Mash 2 tablespoons of the butter with the flour and some salt, pepper and nutmeg until you have a smooth paste. Remove the oysters from the pan and keep warm. Add the liquor from the oysters to the flour paste, stirring to keep it smooth, then make the sauce up to 1½ cups with the milk. Return to the pan, bring to the boil and cook until the sauce thickens. Return the oysters to the sauce, add the remaining butter and adjust the seasoning to taste. Serve as an accompaniment to the steaks.

SERVING VEGETABLES THE FRENCH WAY

"The greatest defect of the English arrangement of dinner is that almost always vegetables are of no account save as adjuncts ... To this rule, however, there are two exceptions made – in favour of artichokes and asparagus. It is a question whether this exception is due to a pure admiration of the vegetable, or to the circumstance that, having to be eaten with the fingers, it is necessary to put down either knife or fork in order to seize the vegetable. The probability is that if the Creator had thought fit, in His wisdom, to endow the Englishman with three or four hands, he would never be seen eating the artichoke or the asparagus alone, but always in conjunction with some other food."

Since Dallas recommends eating both asparagus and artichokes simply boiled with a little butter, I have included a couple of the few other vegetable dishes that he does give.

STUFFED TOMATOES THE FRENCH WAY

Serves 6

INGREDIENTS

6 fairly large tomatoes, the tops removed
3 tablespoons olive oil
2 large garlic cloves, crushed or finely chopped
1 medium onion, finely chopped
salt and pepper
6 tablespoons fresh brown bread crumbs
5 tablespoons chicken or veal stock or mixed white wine and water
2 egg yolks

Remove the flesh from the tomatoes and rub through a coarse strainer to remove the seeds. Then put the flesh in a small pan with the oil, garlic, onion and seasoning and cook gently for 10 minutes, or until the onion is soft. Remove from the heat, add 5 tablespoons of the bread crumbs and the stock or wine mixture and blend thoroughly. Add the egg yolks and mix again. Fill the tomatoes with the mixture, sprinkle the remaining bread crumbs over the top and bake at 375° for 10 minutes. Serve hot, warm or cold.

GREEN PEAS THE FRENCH WAY

Serves 6

INGREDIENTS

3 cups green peas, fresh or frozen
4 tablespoons butter
2 heaped teaspoons all-purpose flour
2 egg yolks
⅔ cup heavy cream
salt and pepper
pinch of sugar

Cook the peas, if frozen, in 2 inches of water, if fresh, in a little more. Drain the peas and keep warm; reserve the water. Melt the butter in a pan and add the flour. Cook for a few minutes, then add about 1 cup of the reserved water. Stir well and cook until the sauce thickens slightly. Turn the heat very low and add the egg yolks and cream; continue to cook very gently for 2 minutes, then season to taste with salt, pepper and sugar and return the peas to the pan. Mix them into the sauce and serve immediately.

QUEEN CHARLOTTE'S PUDDING

Serves 6

Unusually, Dallas makes no comment about this dish. However, one must assume that it was named after George III's wife – at one time the most famous of her name in Europe – to whom Dallas cedes the honor of inspiring the apple Charlotte.

INGREDIENTS

pie crust for 7–8 inch pie plate (page 28)
4 large oranges
2 large lemons
8 large egg yolks
5 tablespoons extra-fine sugar

Roll out the pastry and line a 7–8 inch pie plate; bake it blind and make sure that it is good and crisp. Grate the rinds from the oranges and lemons into a bowl, then squeeze in the juice. Whip the egg yolks and add them to the mixture with the sugar. Pour this into the pastry shell and bake at 300° for 1 hour, or until the filling is set and lightly browned on top. Serve warm or cold.

OMELET WITH RUM

Serves 6

"There is an old philosophic question – Which was produced first, the egg or the hen? Theologians might perhaps decide for the egg, on the grounds that all birds' eggs are innocent and good for food, but all the birds themselves are not. It is difficult to imagine however how the world got on before the barndoor fowl was tamed and taught to lay regularly. The culture of

OMELET WITH RUM (LEFT) AND QUEEN
CHARLOTTE'S PUDDING

the egg is one of the greatest events of civilisation, and has yielded an aliment of the rarest
delicacy, unfailing resource and of magical
variety. . . . The egg may be said to come ready
cooked from the hand of nature – a masterpiece
not easily to be improved upon by mortal
cooks."

I find that the sweet omelet is one of the few
egg dishes where the hand of mortal cook in the
guise of a whisk is an improvement – and the rum
certainly does not detract from it. You can either
make one large omelet in one large pan, in which
case I would not try to turn it but would put it
briefly under a very hot broiler to brown the top,
or two small ones in which case they can be
turned on to a warmed serving dish.

INGREDIENTS

6 medium eggs
6 tablespoons dark rum
4 tablespoons extra-fine sugar
unsalted butter or sunflower oil for
  greasing the pan

Whip the eggs very thoroughly in a bowl with
the sugar and 3 tablespoons of the rum. Heat the
omelet pan with a little butter or sunflower oil
until it is very hot, pour in the egg mixture and
cook as for an ordinary omelet. If you are
making two small omelets it would be better to
cook them both at the same time, then turn them
out on to the serving dish. Sprinkle them with the
remaining sugar, warm the remaining rum, light
it and pour it over the omelets as they are carried
to the table. For one big omelet, sprinkle the
sugar and lighted rum over the omelet in the pan
and carry it straight to the table.

EATING OUT

"One evil of long standing," says *London at Dinner,* the first ever restaurant guide, which came out in 1858, "still exists in London – and that is the difficulty of finding an Hotel or Restaurant where strangers of the gentler sex may be taken to dine. . . . At Greenwich, Hampton Court, Windsor, Slough and Richmond ladies are to be found as in the Parisian cafés, and in London at the 'Epitaux' in Pall Mall, and at 'Verrey's' in Regent Street; but to give a dinner with ladies, it is necessary to take a private room at the 'Albion' or the 'London Tavern.'"

"Eating out" in Victorian times was an almost exclusively male occupation. Of course, there were occasions when ladies had to eat away from home. Traveling might involve staying at inns, but even in the meanest of such hostelries a private room would normally be available for the ladies. Incidentally, the anonymous author of *London at Dinner* recommended an inspection of the larder at country inns before ordering dinner; if you did not approve of what you found, you could visit the butcher or the poulterer to buy your own provisions, with which the host would then prepare your dinner.

Ladies could also, of course, go out to private parties. These were increasingly popular among the "upwardly mobile" Victorian middle classes who frequently beggared themselves in staging immensely elaborate, pretentious, and, all too often, disastrously bad, dinner parties. Similarly, ladies could be seen at public or civic dinners or receptions, dances or balls, the theater or the opera. But at a restaurant – no. As for respectable working women, they could go to fairs and public entertainments and could buy their food from the many city street stalls, but they could not be seen in the public rooms of a tavern or inn. It was not until the latter part of the century, and

THE ST GEORGE'S CLUB IN LONDON

the opening of many small restaurants run by the numerous European refugees who fled to England from 1848 onward (Kettner's, for example) that being seen dining in public ceased to "ruin one's reputation" instantly.

For the men, however, there were a wide range of possibilities. "Dives," the basement or cellar eating houses under many of the public houses, served cheap and basic cow heel, sausages, tripe and bread and butter at communal tables to hackney coachmen, draymen, footmen and gentlemen alike. Upstairs, chops, steaks, vegetables, fruit pies or cheese and beer were usually available, as they had been since the 17th century, for a flat rate charge. Once again they were served at communal tables, but the quality of food and service could be expected to be at least marginally better.

If gentlemen wished to dine in style however, they did so in a restaurant. In London, restaurants such as Simpson's in the Strand, Thomas's, the Albion in Great Russell Street or the St. James's Restaurant in Regent Street were well thought of, as were the restaurants of some of the major hotels. The fame of the turtle soup served at the Adelphi and Waterloo Hotels in Liverpool had even reached the metropolis. Alternatively, and this was probably the more popular option, gentlemen in search of an evening out took a private room in a restaurant or hotel where they could order their dinner in advance and indulge themselves to their hearts' – or stomachs' – content.

By the 19th century there was yet another option available to gentlemen of at least moderate means: the club. Gentlemen's clubs had evolved from 17th century coffee houses where groups with similar interests met and, in due course, formed themselves into small societies. The first actual club, White's, was founded as early as 1696, followed by the Cocoa Tree in 1746, the St. James's in 1757, Boodles in 1762 and Brook's in 1774. However, 18th century clubs were primarily gambling houses for the rich and aristocratic. It was not until the 19th century that they took on their better known guise of dark and comfortable sanctuaries where Victorian man could relax, read his papers, smoke, eat, and indeed live, far from the trials of domestic life.

By the middle of the century there were clubs in every city, to accommodate every shade of opinion, political or religious, every taste and every pocket. Many of the London clubs had built themselves imposing club houses, along Pall Mall or scattered around the West End. Within these hallowed portals, and for a quite modest subscription, members could obtain accommodation, libraries, privacy or good fellowship as required, excellent cellars and food. The latter varied with the club, but in their heyday, chefs such as Alexis Soyer at the Reform Club created meals fit for kings.

New York in the 19th century showed a more relaxed attitude to dining out than did London. The city, which clustered around what is now the financial district at the southern tip of Manhattan, boasted several excellent restaurants, the most famous being Delmonico's in Beaver Street.

The restaurant was started on William Street in 1827 by two Swiss brothers, John and Peter Delmonico, initially as a pastry shop. In 1838 they moved to new premises on Beaver Street (designed for them by John Brown Lord and seating 125 people) and a third brother, Lorenzo, joined them as chef. As New York expanded northward up Manhattan Island, Delmonico's expanded too, opening new branches in select quarters such as the basement of the new building on 14th Street and 5th Avenue, the site of the old Grimaldi mansion. Abraham Lincoln, who lived in the building, was a frequent diner at the restaurant, as was William Seward who purchased Alaska for the United States government. It was in his honor that the chef of the day invented Baked Alaska.

At the height of their success the Delmonico family owned a house in Brooklyn with a garden that stretched for twelve city blocks and in which was grown all the fresh produce served in their restaurants. But the jewel in their crown always remained the Beaver Street restaurant, where their greatest chefs held court. First reigned Lorenzo himself, then Filipi Alessandre and finally the famous chef Charles Ranhofer, who was to produce the American equivalent of Soyer's *Gastronomic Regenerator*.

Ranhofer was born in St. Denis in France in 1836, trained in Paris and in 1856 arrived in America to make his fortune – at Delmonico's. He was to remain at the restaurant, an autocratic and difficult figure, for 34 years, serving presidents, European royalty, literary figures and other notables. Finally, after his retirement he produced, in 1893, his magnum opus, *The Epicurean*. This magnificent work contains over 3,500 recipes; nearly 140 pages of suggested "bills of fare" that cover everything from breakfasts to seated buffets for 400 people; detailed instructions as to table service and "elementary methods" of cooking; advice on seasonality of food and the efficacy of kitchen equipment; and over 800 engraved illustrations that range from simple larding needles to elaborate classical scenes of cherubs and temples recreated from ices or confectionery.

CHAPTER EIGHT

CHRISTMAS DINNER IN THE SERVANTS' HALL

————

Today, to have one living-in servant, is to be wealthy; a hundred years ago quite humble families would expect to have at least one, and often two. In the country, servants were still more numerous as even at the end of the 19th century country dwellers were very self-dependent. It would be nothing unusual to find a medium-size estate such as Erddig, in North Wales, with its own blacksmiths, carpenters, woodmen and foresters, gardeners, housekeepers, cooks, nannies and nursemaids, housemaids, butlers, footmen, coachmen and stable lads, quite apart from any farm workers who might be employed if the estate were farmed.

Erddig was the family seat of the Yorkes, a moderately well-to-do country family. The first Philip Yorke inherited it in 1733 from his uncle, John Meller, whose creation the house had been. Philip's family, in direct line of succession, were to own and live at Erddig until it passed to the National Trust in 1973. During that time the Yorkes maintained an unusually close and intimate relationship with the many staff who worked for them, penning long – and frequently poetically painful – verses in their praise. They also had portraits painted of many of the staff and hung in the house, flanked by their eulogies:

"Ruth Jones of whom we now make mention
Is worthy of our best attention
Like one of whom 'tis here recorded
In terms jocose and quaintly worded
That 'seventy years or nigh had past her
Since spider-brusher to the Master';
Tho' not like her with coachman mated
But to our Keeper thus related

————

OPPOSITE: OXTAIL SOUP AND POTTED HAM

Ruth did the former record break,
For she did here her entry make
As early books of wages show,
Full one and seventy years ago;
As housemaid then for lengthy space
She was a credit to her race,
And 'midst a group her face appears
When younger by some threescore years . . ."

The Yorkes did not pay particularly well – indeed wages at Erddig were low compared to other similar size houses – but the "fringe benefits" of working for the family were considerable: pensions and often a cottage on the estate when they retired, extra gifts and presents during their working life, comfortable quarters and good food. As a result the majority of their staff remained with the family for life, often marrying within the estate. The layout of the house (all of which can now be seen, beautifully restored) was also condusive to master/servant familiarity. The kitchens were only separated from the dining-room and saloon by a door, the servants' hall looked out over the garden and the billiard room was in the basement in the middle of the servants' quarters.

That all of this has survived intact is thanks to the late Simon and Philip Yorke; the former lived at Erddig from 1922 until 1966, adamantly refusing to allow any repairs or alterations to be made to the house. As a result, Philip Yorke inherited it in 1966 in an appalling state of disrepair. After prolonged and tortuous negotiations he gave the estate to the National Trust and did much to help in its subsequent transformation. The story is fascinating and the house well worth a visit.

Christmas celebrations at Erddig, as in similar country houses, would have been prolonged,

— 99 —

stretching over one or two weeks from Christmas Eve or St. Nicholas's Eve through until Twelfth Night on January 6. The family would often have guests over this period, and although it was still the custom for guests to bring gifts of food with them if coming for a long stay, there would still have been much for the cook and her minions to do. With no refrigeration, food had to be prepared that would keep well in a cool larder over the whole holiday. Hence the popularity of dishes such as spiced beef and potted ham, both of which could be relied on to keep fresh for a couple of weeks.

The servants would of course have worked all over the Christmas holiday but it is likely that in a family such as the Yorkes, time would have been allowed for them to hold their own Christmas celebrations. The more exotic dishes such as the goose and the boar's head would have been reserved for the family, but traditional roasts of beef, soups, puddings and pies would certainly have graced the servants' hall board.

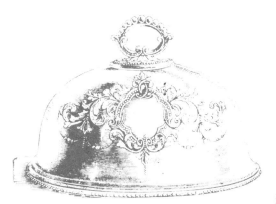

OXTAIL SOUP

Serves 10

A good pot of soup was always welcome on a wintry Christmas Day, both for its warming qualities and because it helped to fill an empty stomach that might not get as much meat as it would hope – even at Christmas! On any other day a rich soup like this would almost make a meal in itself.

INGREDIENTS

2¼ lb oxtail, cut up
3 quarts cold water
1 teaspoon salt
handful of peppercorns
2 onions, stuck with 6 cloves each
3 large carrots, thickly sliced
handful of parsley with plenty of stalks

Put the oxtail pieces into a large pan and cover them with the cold water. Bring them fairly rapidly to a boil and skim off any scum that rises. Add the salt and continue to skim until all the scum has been removed. Add the peppercorns, onions, carrots and parsley, cover the pan and simmer gently for 3 to 4 hours, or until the meat has fallen off the bones. Alternatively, cook the oxtail pieces in a slow cookpot overnight.

Remove the oxtail pieces and discard all the bones; cut the meat, if necessary, into bite-size pieces. Discard the parsley and remove the cloves from the onions. Chop the onions roughly, return them to the stock, with the meat, and leave to cool. When quite cold, remove the excess fat. Reheat the soup and adjust the seasoning to taste before serving with lots of fresh rough brown bread.

POTTED HAM

Serves 10 as a starter

This would normally have been made from the leftovers of a piece of ham and veal – a good way of using it up before it went off. If you don"t have any leftovers, you can start from scratch. The veal was originally added to tone down the saltiness of the ham, but even if your ham is not very salty, I think that the veal makes the final product more interesting. The recipe, which is Eliza Acton's, insists that the meats be very thoroughly pounded with the butter in a pestle and mortar, and I am afraid that this is one occasion when modern gadgets cannot be substituted. A food processor, grinder or blender will tear the fibers of the meat, which produces a quite different, and far less satisfactory, result.

INGREDIENTS

1 lb cooked ham off the bone, very well
  trimmed
about ¼ lb roast veal
2 sticks plus 4 tablespoons unsalted
  butter
about 1 teaspoon mace
about ½ teaspoon nutmeg
about ½ teaspoon cayenne pepper

Note   If you do not have any roast veal and cannot easily buy it ready cooked, buy about ½ lb uncooked stewing veal, trim it and bake it in a small dish, covered with foil for 25 minutes, then allow to cool completely.

Chop the meats as small as you can with a very sharp knife. Pound them in a mortar with two sticks of the butter and the spices until you have a relatively smooth paste. How smooth you make it will depend on your own taste and energy level. Add more spices if you feel they are necessary. When it is ready, press the mixture down well into a pot. Clarify the remaining butter and allow it to cool to lukewarm before pouring over the meat to seal it. Eliza says that "if kept in a cool, dry place, this meat will remain good for a fortnight or more."

SPICED BEEF

Serves 10

The beef will take at least twelve days to spice properly and should keep for two weeks after it is cooked, if it is stored in a cool place. It can be eaten hot with the juices in which it was cooked, or cold with salads and potatoes. In a Victorian household a huge roast of 12–15 pounds would have been used; I have reduced that to more modest, 20th century proportions.

INGREDIENTS

1 teaspoon mace
1 teaspoon black pepper
1 heaped teaspoon cloves
1 heaped teaspoon nutmeg
½ teaspoon cayenne
⅔ cup raw cane sugar
about 4½ lb round, rump, or flank of
  beef
scant ⅓ cup salt
2½–5 cups beef or veal stock
1 medium onion
4 small carrots
large sprig of fresh parsley
2 sprigs of fresh thyme or 1 teaspoon
  dried

Mix the spices thoroughly with the sugar and rub the mixture well into the beef. Put it in a large porcelain, glass or stainless-steel dish, cover it lightly and leave it for three days in a cool place – a larder is ideal. Rub in the salt and leave the beef for a further ten to twelve days, turning it every 24 hours. Do not worry if it gets a little "rusty," just rub it well with the pickle mixture and turn it well in it.

To cook, wash but do not soak the beef, tie it into a good shape if necessary, then put it into a pan as near its own size as you can manage. Pour in sufficient stock to come two thirds of the way up the meat, bring it to a boil and skim off any scum that may rise. Add the onion, carrots, parsley and thyme, cover and simmer very gently for 3 to 4 hours, or cook it in a slow cooker overnight. Serve the beef hot, with its juices (seasoned to taste if necessary), or allow to cool in its juices and serve cold. The cooking juices, diluted, make an excellent soup.

"A BOILED TURKEY"

Serves 10

Although they were not a traditional Christmas dish, turkeys had become popular as the center-piece of the Christmas meal by the end of Victoria's reign. This recipe is from Alexis Soyer's *Shilling Cookery* so would have been well suited to the servants' hall.

INGREDIENTS

1 small (4½ lb) turkey
½ cup ground beef suet or shortening
4½ cups fresh whole-wheat bread crumbs
1 teaspoon salt
¼ teaspoon pepper
1 teaspoon dried thyme
grated rind of 1 lemon
3 eggs
about 1 lb bacon or salt pork, cut in largish pieces
2 onions, roughly chopped
3 celery stalks, roughly chopped
6 peppercorns
3 bouquets garnis
2 tablespoons butter
½ cup whole-wheat flour
1¼ cups milk

Remove any giblets and such like from the bird. Mix the suet, bread crumbs, salt, pepper, thyme, lemon rind and eggs thoroughly in a bowl and use it to stuff both ends of the turkey, securing where necessary with a skewer. Lower the bird into a pan just big enough to hold it and surround with the bacon pieces, onions and celery. Add the peppercorns and bouquets garnis, then cover with water. Bring to a boil and simmer gently for 1½ hours. Cool in the cooking liquid. When the turkey is quite cold, take it out of the pan and re-move the fat from the cooking juices.

Melt the butter in a separate pan and add the flour; cook for a minute or two. Add 2 cups of the strained liquor from the pot gradually, then the milk. Cook until the sauce thickens slightly. Strain the remaining stock and reserve it. Chop up the cooked onions and celery and add them to the sauce. You can also chop up the bacon and add it, or you can serve the pieces separately with the turkey. Season the sauce to taste.

To serve the turkey, replace it in the pot with the reserved stock and bring back to a boil very gently. Simmer for 10 to 15 minutes to make sure it is heated right through. Reheat the sauce. Re-move the turkey very carefully – it should be tender enough to fall apart – to a serving dish. Arrange the bacon pieces around it, if you are serving them that way, and pour over some of the sauce; serve the rest separately. Serve with plenty of freshly boiled or steamed root vegetables and maybe some stewed cabbage (page 42).

OPPOSITE: BOILED TURKEY SERVED WITH STEAMED ROOT VEGETABLES AND SAUCE

CHRISTMAS PLUM PUDDING
Serves 10

Victorian Christmas puddings were usually boiled in a cloth rather than in a bowl so that they emerged theoretically quite circular, but the mixture can equally be steamed in a bowl in the conventional way. This recipe, which makes a relatively light pudding but "a very good one" is from Mrs. Beeton's *New and Enlarged Cookery Book* of 1894. She suggests making the pudding "a few days before it is required for the table," but you can make it further in advance if you wish.

INGREDIENTS

3 cups raisins
¾ cup currants
⅔ cup mixed candied fruit peel
4 cups brown bread crumbs
1 cup ground suet
6 eggs
½ cup, plus 1 tablespoon, brandy

Mix the dry ingredients together thoroughly. Beat the eggs with the ½ cup of brandy and mix into the dry ingredients. If the pudding is to be steamed, press the mixture down into a buttered bowl and cover with foil or wax paper, held in place with string or a rubber band. Put the bowl into a pan, add water until it comes two thirds up the sides of the bowl, cover the pan and steam for 4 hours. If the pudding is to be cooked in a cloth, tie up the pudding securely but not too tightly, submerge it in a deep pan of boiling water, bring to a boil, cover and boil gently for 4 hours.

If the pudding was cooked in a bowl, it can be left to cool and merely re-steamed for 2 hours before serving. If it was cooked in a cloth, take it out of the water and hang it up to drain and cool; to reheat, boil as before for a further 2 hours. In either case, turn the pudding out on to a heated plate and pour round the tablespoon of brandy, which should be lit just as it is carried to the table. Serve with brandy sauce (below).

BRANDY SAUCE

INGREDIENTS

1 stick butter
2 teaspoons whole-wheat or all-purpose
  flour
1¼ cups water
2 tablespoons extra-fine sugar
½ cup brandy

Melt the butter with the flour and add the water immediately. Cook all together for a few minutes, then add the sugar and the brandy. Bring the sauce back to boiling point but do not let it boil. Serve very hot with the Christmas pudding (above).

MINCE PIES

Makes about 20–30 pies

This recipe comes from the Erddig manuscript cookbooks and dates from the late 18th or early 19th century. You will notice that it contains a very high proportion of apple – and some chopped tongue. Originally, mince pies were ground meat pies cooked with dried fruits to help to preserve them. Gradually the fruits took over until, by the late Victorian period, the meat had all but disappeared.

INGREDIENTS

4 cups whole-wheat flour
scant 2 sticks butter or butter and lard
    mixed
½ cup ground beef suet
⅔ cup currants
¼ cup extra-fine sugar
2 cups coarsely grated apple
¼ cup raisins
⅓ cup finely chopped cold tongue, or
    "salt boiled beef"
½ teaspoon grated nutmeg
½ teaspoon cloves
½ teaspoon mace
rind and juice of 1 Seville orange (if
    obtainable), 1 small orange and 1
    small lemon, or rind and juice of 1
    orange, 1 lemon and 1 lime
⅓ cup candied orange or lemon peel
    (optional)
2 tablespoons brandy or orange brandy

Rub the fat into the flour and mix to a stiff paste with cold water. Roll out the pastry and use to line small patty or tartlet pans, reserving enough pastry for the lids.

Mix all the remaining ingredients together thoroughly, then fill the patty pans. Cover each with a pastry lid, pierce it to let the steam out and bake at 375° for 15 to 20 minutes, or until the pastry is browned and firm. Remove from the pans as soon as possible and leave to cool on a wire rack. Serve warm or cold.

PLUM CAKE

This recipe is dated 1890 and comes from the Erddig manuscript cookbooks. The mixture would make two 8 inch cakes or one 12 inch one. It is better if made several weeks, or even months, before it is needed. If so, it should be wrapped in foil and stored, in an airtight tin, in a cool place. The manuscript gives no directions for icing the cake but if you want to do so, use almond paste and white frosting.

INGREDIENTS

3 sticks soft butter
1¼ cups raw cane sugar
4 tablespoons molasses
6 eggs
1¼ cups warmed milk
2 teaspoons vanilla extract
4 cups flour, whole-wheat or half
    whole-wheat and half all-purpose
2⅔ cups currants
3 cups golden raisins
1⅓ cups candied fruit peel

Beat the butter to a cream with the sugar. Warm the molasses slightly, then add it to the butter mixture. Add one egg at a time, with a spoonful of flour between each, and beat thoroughly. Then add the milk and vanilla with a further spoonful of flour and beat again. Mix in the remaining flour and the fruits. Spoon into a well-buttered pan (lined with parchment paper unless it has a removable base). Bake at 325° for 1¾ hours if you are making the smaller cakes, for 2¼ hours if you are making the large one. Test with a skewer to make sure it is cooked. Remove from the oven and allow to cool in the pan. When quite cold, wrap and store till needed.

OVERLEAF: PLUM CAKE (LEFT), CHRISTMAS PLUM PUDDING WITH BRANDY SAUCE (TOP) AND MINCE PIES

ENTERTAINING
ON THE GRAND SCALE

On May 29, 1867, Lord Warkworth, grandson of the 5th Duke of Northumberland, and heir to one of the greatest estates in England, came of age. Even today such events do not go unnoticed; in the middle of Victoria's reign they were cause for mighty celebration.

In the Northumberland family archives at Syon House, a commonplace book, lovingly put together by an anonymous retainer, records the events of that momentous week, mainly through the reports in the local press. First came the actual birthday celebrations on May 29 culminating in a dinner for all sixteen hundred and fifty of the Alnwick tenantry. The reporter from the *Newcastle Daily Chronicle* was inspired: "The morning dawned with the most auspicious auguries for weather favourable to the outdoor proceedings on the long looked for day on which the coming of age of Lord Warkworth, the young heir of the ancient House of Percy, was to be celebrated at Alnwick. A heavy squall of wind and a smart shower shortly after daybreak served to freshen the air, and in due time glorious Sol arose in all the grandeur of early summer to commence his diurnal course. Brightly fell his rays over the yet sleeping town, over the slumbering woodlands of the Parks, the Pastures and the Dairy Ground, encircling with their wooded masses of·many tinted greens the princely castle of the Percies . . ."

And so he went on, for a further eight columns, describing the presentation of the addresses to Lord Warkworth, and his replies; the inspection of the state apartments of the castle; the review of the volunteers and distribution of "Challenge Medals;" the dinner given to the volunteers and then, the great event of the day, the dinner served to the tenantry, to music supplied by the Northumberland Infantry Militia Band. So impressed was the reporter that before he went on to detail all the speeches which were made in Lord Warkworth's honor at the dinner – and his gracious replies – he listed the dishes that were served (by one hundred and sixty waiters, each of whom was provided with a card to confirm his engagement for the evening)

to the guests in the coach-house and covered stableyard:

◆

60 salmon	50 turbots
50 dressed fish	50 fried soles
2 barons of beef	2 cold barons of beef
30 haunch of venison	30 necks of venison
20 pieces of roast beef	20 haunches of mutton
30 boiled legs of mutton	76 boiled fowls
50 salmon with salad	150 roast chickens
25 hams	40 tongues
24 rounds of beef	36 raised pies
36 roasts of lamb	18 ballotines of lamb
24 savory jellies	24 pressed veal
128 plum puddings	100 fruit tarts
150 pastries, various	100 jellies
60 creams	25 savory cakes
25 nougats	25 Neapolitan cakes
25 babas	25 meringues
25 Orleans puddings	

◆

The Alnwick staff were numerous and experienced but even they must have found such quantities somewhat daunting. But, this was only the beginning. The following day, a Thursday, it was the children's turn. Luncheon was served to two hundred of the local children (who once again drank the health of Lord Warkworth who, once again, graciously replied) in the same stableyard, after which the afternoon was spent in games and sports in the castle grounds.

On Friday the Grand Ball was held, attended by the gentry from miles around. Once again the reporter waxed lyrical:
"It is hardly within the scope of writing, boundless as that scope is considered by many, and great as are the liberties that are often taken with it, correctly and succinctly to describe the extraordinary state of excitement in which are the inhabitants of Alnwick tonight."

ONE OF 160 WAITER'S TICKETS FOR THE
ALNWICK CELEBRATIONS

Due to the press of guests and a certain shortage of conveyances, proceedings were somewhat delayed and the dancing did not get properly under way, under the guidance of Mr. Hemy and his band, until after 9 pm. However, despite the delay and the reporter's opinion that "the musical programme was rather high for popular taste," he had to admit that "the floor was one animated and symmetrical maze of dancers" cavorting themselves with much grace and enthusiasm until "the silver trumpet blew for supper." This time he does not regale us with the menu, but he comments that "once again the culinary genius of Mr. Thorpe and the provident forethought and organising capacity of Mr. R. Pantling and Mr. G. Alderson were conspicuous."

Not only were their culinary genius and provident forethought impressive, but their stamina was quite amazing. The official program finished at 3 am but so good a time was being had by all, that the remaining guests and the servants who had just come off duty, persuaded Messrs. Pantling and Alderson to perform on the cornet, to the accompaniment of Mr. Hemy's indefatigable band, so that the dancing could continue till sunrise.

And back on duty they were the following morning, the stableyard cleared of the paraphernalia of the ball, the tables decorated with hothouse plants, Mr. Hemy and his band once more at the ready, to serve a midday dinner to three hundred and fifty of the workmen on the estate and those who had helped with the events of the previous three days. By then, even the reporter was running out of literary steam, but he does note that the "dinner and dessert were excellent," and that "there was a plentiful supply of choice wines" – and of course, Lord Warkworth's health was once again drunk, and, once again, he graciously replied . . .

Sunday was a day of rest.

GRAND DINNER AT ALNWICK CASTLE

CHAPTER NINE

A CELEBRATION OF HARVEST HOME

The life of a farm laborer in the Victorian era was not a happy one. With very few exceptions they were miserably poor, sickly, overworked, and half starved. In some areas of the country a few laborers still had enough land around their cottages to keep a pig, or occasionally a cow, and some hens, and to grow a few vegetables or fruits. But the 18th century agricultural revolution had allowed the large farmers to "enclose" much of the "common land" into arable and pasture fields, thereby depriving most of the small cottagers of their right to graze their pig or their cow. Even when a small piece of ground was still available, so many of the women and children were also employed to work in the fields, especially in the early years of the century, that there was no one at home to care for their own little allotment. The wages earned by the women and children were pitifully low. As the century wore on, the use of female and child labor declined – but by then, many of the traditional housewifely skills had been lost.

Well into the 20th century farm workers in the north of England and in Scotland still received part of their wages in kind, so they were guaranteed at least a basic diet of oatmeal, milk and vegetables, with the occasional piece of meat. On some farms in the south and east of England the men were fed by the farmer and the cost of their food deducted from their already meager wages. This was fine for the men as they got at least one reasonable meal per day, but since almost half their wages might be deducted to pay for their food, it was hard on the wife who had to feed herself and the children on what was left. The result was that most families lived almost entirely on bread, potatoes, a little bit of butter, tea with a little sugar and occasionally, if they were lucky, a little cheese, bacon or milk. Vegetables were rarely seen and a family would think itself lucky if it had one hot meal each week.

It is not hard to imagine, therefore, how welcome the occasional harvest feast must have been. Toward the end of the century such feasts were becoming rare – many had degenerated into Sunday events on the village green, with singing in the church and tea and cake in the village schoolroom. But in the early years of Victoria's reign the arrival of the last loads of corn in the barns or stackyards was still celebrated with gargantuan feasts in the large farmhouse kitchens. Workers, their wives and their families would stuff themselves to bursting – and beyond – with all the food they would be unlikely to see again for a year. Richard Cobbold, in his novel *Margaret Catchpole*, which was published in 1845, describes one such feast, though the apparent air of bonhomie may have owed more to the novelist's imagination than the real world:

"One pair of hands could not, indeed, have prepared sufficient eatables for such a party – smoking puddings, plain and plum; piles of hot potatoes, cabbages, turnips, carrots and every species of vegetable which the farmer's lands could produce – beef, roast and boiled, mutton, veal, and pork, everything good and substantial (the food that normally graced the farmer's own bounteous table); a rich custard and apple pies to which the children did ample justice, for all were seated around this well furnished table in the old kitchen.

"The lord of the feast, or head man in the harvest field, took his station at the head of the table, whilst the master of the house, his sister and even his daughter, were the servants of the feast and took every pain to satisfy and gratify the party. After the feast, and a flowing jug or two of

---

OPPOSITE: BOILED LEG OF MUTTON WITH OX TONGUE AND CUCUMBER SAUCE

brown ale had been emptied, the wives and children were invited into the best parlour to tea and cakes, whilst the merry reapers were left to themselves to enjoy in their own way the stronger harvest ale, which was just broached by the hand of their master."

The vegetables to which Cobbold refers would all have been boiled, so just use as many as you can fit in, avoiding obviously tropical ones which would not have been available in the Victorian countryside.

BOILED LEG OF MUTTON WITH TURNIPS

Serves 10

This recipe is Eliza Acton's and, as she points out, it needs long, slow cooking to get the best results. The broth in which the meat is simmered makes excellent soup, which would no doubt have been appreciated by the farm workers although they might not have bothered with the cucumber sauce that Eliza recommends (and I am including) to go with it. She also suggests that a small ox-tongue "boiled very tender" might make a good accompaniment to the mutton, and I am sure that the harvesters would have agreed.

INGREDIENTS

a good sized (5–6 lb) leg of mutton or
*   mature lamb*
about 3¾ quarts veal, chicken or lamb
*   stock or water*
1 tablespoon salt
2 onions, with 8 cloves stuck in them
4–5 large carrots, thickly sliced
2 bouquets garnis
5–6 medium sized turnips, quartered

Put the meat into a large heavy pan and add enough of the cold stock or water to cover it fairly generously. Bring to a boil reasonably fast and remove any scum. Add the salt, which will encourage the scum to rise, and continue to cook reasonably fast until most of the scum has been removed. Add the onions, carrots and herbs and cook gently for 30 minutes. Add the turnips, cover the pan and simmer very gently for 3 hours. Allow to cool completely and then remove any fat. To serve, reheat the meat very gently in the cooking juices, then remove to a serving dish and "bring to the table" accompanied by the cucumber sauce (below).

CUCUMBER SAUCE

INGREDIENTS

6 inch piece of cucumber, peeled,
*   halved lengthwise and cut in thin*
*   slices*
3 tablespoons seasoned whole-wheat
*   flour*
4 tablespoons butter
1 large onion, minced fine
2 cups good brown gravy or juices from
*   cooking the lamb or mutton*
2 tablespoons red wine vinegar
salt and pepper

Note   If you substitute equal quantities of milk and cream for the gravy, this also makes an excellent sauce for fish.

Toss the cucumber thoroughly in the seasoned flour. Melt the butter in a wide pan, add the cucumber, remaining flour and onion and cook them all briskly until they are well colored. Add the gravy or juices gradually, making sure that you incorporate all the burned bits of roux off the bottom of the pan. Simmer for 5 minutes, then add the vinegar and seasoning to taste. Serve, hot, with the lamb or mutton (above).

BEEFSTEAK PUDDING

Serves 10

Among the steaming puddings on the board would have been a beefsteak one, complete with kidneys and a few mushrooms. This recipe comes from the 1894 edition of Mrs. Beeton and she notes that it "was contributed by a Sussex lady, in which county the inhabitants are noted for their savoury puddings." You will need a large bowl or casserole and a saucepan large enough to hold it.

INGREDIENTS

4¼ cups whole-wheat flour
1 cup ground beef suet
2 lb well trimmed braising beef
1 lb well trimmed kidney (optional)
2¼ cups mushrooms, halved or
* quartered according to size*
3-4 tablespoons well seasoned whole-
* wheat flour*

Note   If you do not want to use the kidney increase the beef to 3 lb.

Mix the flour with the suet and add sufficient water gradually to make a firm paste. Roll this out and line a bowl or casserole large enough to hold all the meat – you should leave enough paste hanging over the edge to fold over and cover the pudding.

Toss the meat and mushrooms thoroughly in the seasoned flour, then layer them in the bowl, seasoning generously between each layer. Add water to within 2 inches of the top, then fold over the paste. If there is not enough to cover the pudding, use leftover scraps to patch the top. Cover the bowl with wax paper or foil, tied down with string or a rubber band. Put it in the pan and add water until it comes two thirds of the way up the bowl. Cover the saucepan and boil briskly for 4 hours. Remove the bowl from the pan, take off the covering and cut the paste out of the top to reveal the steak. Serve immediately.

If you want to make it in advance, do not uncover the pudding after it is cooked but reheat it by reboiling for 1 hour or by putting it in a microwave for 6 to 8 minutes.

CABBAGE STEWED WITH BACON

Serves 10

This was a dish which the farm laborer no doubt often wished he could eat on Sunday – but seldom did. The recipe is from Soyer's *Shilling Cookery* and, although it is very simple, it tastes excellent.

INGREDIENTS

3 large onions, roughly chopped
1 very large or 2 medium Savoy
* cabbages, fairly thinly sliced*
piece of bacon, weighing about 3 lb
6 cloves
handful of black peppercorns
3–4 bay leaves
2 sprigs of parsley
about 5 cups water

Note   Because of the saltiness of the bacon, do not add any salt.

Mix the onions into the cabbage and lay half in the bottom of a large, ovenproof casserole. Place the piece of bacon on top and sprinkle over the cloves, peppercorns, bay leaves and parsley. Cover with the remaining cabbage mixture and pour over the water. Cover the pot tightly and bake at 350° for 2 hours. Remove the bacon on to a serving dish and surround with the cabbage and juices; serve immediately with plenty of potatoes to mop up the juices.

JUGGED HARE

Serves 8 to 10

The hunting of game was restricted to the land-owners, with fearsome penalties if you were caught poaching, so a rich hare, cooked in its own blood, would have been a rare treat. To jug the hare properly you will need a casserole or "jug" large enough to fit the hare and a saucepan large enough to fit the casserole so that it can be boiled like a steamed pudding. If necessary, you can divide the mixture in half and cook it in two smaller pots and pans.

INGREDIENTS

1 hare, cleaned and cut in large pieces
the blood from the hare if possible
salt and pepper
¼ lb fat bacon, in a piece if possible,
 chopped
3 small onions, roughly chopped
rind of 1 lemon, thinly pared
2 teaspoons chopped dried or fresh
 thyme
2 teaspoons chopped parsley
2 teaspoons fresh chopped or 1 teaspoon
 dried marjoram
½ teaspoon ground mace
½ teaspoon ground cloves
½ teaspoon ground nutmeg
1 cup rough red wine
1 cup good beef, veal or chicken stock
juice of 2 Seville oranges or 1 small
 orange and ½ lemon
2 tablespoons butter (optional)
¼ cup whole-wheat flour (optional)
slices of lemon
red currant jelly

Season the pieces of hare thoroughly and put them into a jug or casserole, layered with the bacon, onions, lemon rind, herbs and spices. Mix the blood with the red wine, stock and citrus fruit juice and pour over the hare. Cover the jug or casserole, using foil to make a good seal under the lid, put it into a saucepan and fill it two thirds up the sides of the casserole with water. Bring to

a boil and cook for 3 to 4 hours, always keeping the water at a gentle boil. The hare can then be served straight from the jug or casserole. Alternatively, the hare could be cooked in a slow cooker overnight and served directly from the pot. If you prefer the hare without bones and with a thicker sauce, remove the pieces of hare from the jug and bone them. Strain the cooking juices and thicken the sauce with the butter and flour mixed together thoroughly and cook gently until the sauce thickens. Return the sauce to the jug with the hare and reheat gently, but do not allow the water to boil. Adjust the seasoning to taste and serve it hot with slices of lemon and red currant jelly.

ROAST PORK WITH APPLE SAUCE

Serves 10

Although a bit of bacon was the only kind of meat that most farm workers ever saw, a large roast of pork, inches deep in crackling would have been a very different, and much more appealing, dish. The sauce is Eliza Acton's as she insists, rightly, that sauce made with baked rather than boiled apples is "far superior."

INGREDIENTS

about 6 lb leg of pork with its rind well
 scored
3 lb cooking or tart eating apples
3 tablespoons water
2–4 tablespoons extra-fine sugar
4 tablespoons butter

Roast the pork at 350°, allowing 25 minutes per pound.

Meanwhile, peel, core and slice the apples thickly. Put them into an ovenproof dish with the water, and bake, covered, with the pork, for about 1 hour, or until they are totally mushed. Remove the apples from the oven and beat with a wooden spoon until they are smooth, adding the butter and sugar to taste. Serve, piping hot, with the pork.

OPPOSITE: ROAST PORK WITH APPLE SAUCE AND (TOP) JUGGED HARE

APPLE PIE AND CUSTARD
Serves 10

A deep apple pie with a thick, rich, buttery crust and lots of custard, or cream, would have gone down particularly well with the children. If you want to reproduce the original faithfully, be generous with the pastry which should be thick and crisp. The custard recipe (right) is one of Mrs. Beeton's.

INGREDIENTS

2 sticks plus 2 tablespoons butter
4 cups whole-wheat flour, or mixed
  whole-wheat and all-purpose
7–8 lb cooking or tart eating apples,
  peeled and thickly sliced
¼–½ cup extra-fine sugar, depending
  on the variety of apple and how
  sweet you like your puddings
⅔ cup water

Cut and rub the butter into the flour and mix to a stiff dough with cold water. Pile the apples into a large pie dish – if you do not have one big enough, use two – sprinkling the layers with the sugar and making sure that the apples are well piled up in the middle. Add the water. Roll out the pastry and cover the dish or dishes, putting a thin strip of paste round the rim before laying on the main lid. Cut a couple of slits in the top of the pie and decorate with little pastry balls made from the trimmings. Bake at 350° for 40 to 45 minutes, or until the pastry is brown and crisp. Remove from the oven and sprinkle with a little extra sugar. Serve hot or warm with rich custard (right), although the leftovers will be excellent cold.

RICH CUSTARD

Mrs. Beeton's recipe does not use cornstarch but does have a nasty habit of curdling when you are not looking. If you do not want to live dangerously, add a little cornstarch to stabilize the mixture. If you use cornstarch you should be able to make the custard in advance and just keep it warm in a double boiler until you need it. Isabella actually allows 8 eggs to 2½ cups of milk, but they would have been smaller than modern eggs.

INGREDIENTS

4 whole eggs and 4 egg yolks
2 tablespoons extra-fine sugar
3 teaspoons cornstarch (optional)
2 drops of vanilla extract
3¾ cups milk
2 tablespoons brandy (optional)

Beat the eggs and egg yolks thoroughly, then mix in the sugar and cornstarch, if you are using it, to make a smooth paste. Add the vanilla extract and pour the mixture into the top of a double boiler or a bowl over a pan of boiling water. Heat the milk to almost boiling point, then add it gradually to the egg mixture, stirring all the time. Keep the water in the pan boiling gently and continue to stir until the custard thickens. Add the brandy and serve with the apple pie (left).

CHEESECAKE

Serves 10

Even at the end of the 19th century most farms still made their own butter and cheese in their own dairy, so cheesecakes, made from fresh new milk, were a familiar luxury. You should be able to use pasteurized milk quite successfully.

INGREDIENTS

2½ quarts fresh milk – the creamier the better
2 tablespoons rennet
puff pastry for a 9–10 inch deep pie dish (page 127)
½ cup extra-fine sugar
⅓ cup melted butter
4 egg yolks
½ teaspoon freshly grated (if possible) nutmeg
grated rind and juice of 1 lemon
½ cup brandy
⅓ cup raisins

Heat the milk to lukewarm, pour it into a bowl and add the rennet. Cover the bowl and leave it in a warm place for at least 1 hour. Break up the curd with your hand, cover the bowl again and leave for another 30 minutes. Let the curd drip through a strainer for 12 to 24 hours, stirring it with a spoon occasionally to release all the whey, which can either be discarded or drunk.

When you are ready to make the cheesecake, roll out the pastry and line a deep 9–10 inch pie dish; bake it blind until crisp.

Beat the curd in a bowl with the sugar, butter, egg yolks, nutmeg, lemon rind and juice, and brandy. Make the mixture as smooth as you can, then rub it through a coarse strainer. Add the raisins and pour the mixture into the pie dish. Bake at 250° for 1 hour. Don't worry if the mixture curdles slightly – it still tastes excellent. Serve warm or cool with extra cream if you like.

APPLE BATTER

Serves 10

This kind of batter, without the sugar, was used to make the boiled bacon and batter puddings that formed the staple food of many a farm family through the week. One can see how it would have provided a good filling meal – but I find the apple version more appealing.

INGREDIENTS

10 medium-sized tart eating apples, or 5 large tart cooking apples, peeled and cored
about ⅔ cup raw cane sugar
2 cups flour, all whole-wheat or half whole-wheat and half all-purpose, depending on how "bready" a pudding you like
4 medium eggs
½ teaspoon salt
2½ cups milk
1¼–2 cups heavy cream

Fill the center of each apple with sugar and pack the fruit fairly tightly in a well-buttered oven-proof pie dish. Beat the flour with the eggs, salt, the remaining tablespoon of sugar and the milk in a blender, food processor or mixer until you have a smooth batter. Pour this over the apples and bake them at 350° for 45 minutes, or until the apples are cooked and the batter risen and browned. Serve immediately with lots of cream.

OVERLEAF: CHEESECAKE (LEFT), APPLE PIE AND CUSTARD (RIGHT) AND APPLE BATTER

FARMING AND KITCHEN GARDENS

Agriculture is notoriously conservative. Although in the latter years of the 19th century, scientists were producing new theories and techniques at a prodigious rate, it was only the advanced minority of landowners who paid any serious attention to them. The vast majority of small farmers (whose holdings usually ranged from thirty to three hundred acres) continued in the old – and all too often, inefficient – way, taking little notice of the innovations adopted by their wealthier neighbors.

However, there certainly was experimentation, led from on high. Following in the footsteps of George III, Prince Albert was a keen and enthusiastic farmer. A member of the Smithfield Club and Highland Agricultural Society, he was also a founder member of the Royal Agricultural Society and implemented many reforms on the royal estates. He insisted on a livestock section at the Great Exhibition of 1851 (where he showed a shorthorn bull and two Suffolk boars); he built roads, drained and then planted trees all over Windsor Great Park and substantially increased the farm holdings at most of the other royal palaces. Balmoral and Osborne especially benefited from his attention where wretched and over-used land was cleaned, fallowed, limed and put down to grass.

In his wake came a band of gentleman farmers such as Henry Handley of Culverthorpe Hall, Charles Hillyard of Thorpelands (whose manual

NEW FARM EQUIPMENT, 1886

Practical farming and grazing with observations on the breeding and feeding of cattle and sheep, published in 1837, was widely read), and Captain Turnhill of Reasbly in Lincolnshire, all eager to try new methods. These men drained their lands and experimented with chalk, bones, lime and the new chemical fertilizers. They bought and used the new machines that, with the arrival of the steam engine, proliferated. They fed oilcake to their stock overwintered in yards, thus achieving large quantities of rich manure. And they prospered.

The chemical fertilizer industry really got under way in 1840. Not that the idea was anything new. Waste products of one kind or another had been in use since the 16th century, but although their efficacy was recognized, little was understood about how they worked. In 1840 however, the German Professor Leibig (Eliza Acton's master, of soup and essence fame) published a report on *The State of Organic Chemistry and Organic Analysis,* in which he proved that plants needed more than the natural

CULTIVATING A FIELD, 1860

organic humus to be found in the soil for good health; carbon and nitrogen were essential outside elements.

Leibig attempted to market the results of his discoveries in the form of a chemical manure, but since he did not include a source of nitrogen, such as ammonia, his manure did not work. However, his ideas were adopted and developed by a young Hertfordshire farmer, John Lawes, who engaged Joseph Gilbert, a chemical assistant who had been trained at Leibig's laboratory at Geissen. Together they laid the foundations of the now famous Rothamsted Experimental Station to test the scientists' chemical discoveries and develop these on a practical scale.

During the same period much progress was also made in animal husbandry. The oil byproducts of seeds – cotton, linseed and so on – were used to make cakes and concentrates that enormously increased the range of winter foodstuffs available.

Most of these developments took place between the 1840s and the 1880s – a period of agricultural boom in England. The early years of the century had seen very hard times. Bad harvests and disastrous crop failures, added to the restrictive Corn Laws and debilitating effects of the Poor Law system, had caused considerable suffering and near starvation in many parts of rural England. However, the reform of the Poor Laws in the 1830s and finally, the repeal of the Corn Laws after the rioting and near revolution caused by the agricultural disasters of 1845, were the turning point. For the next forty years good summers and excellent harvests, combined with the industrial expansion which drew the poorest laborers to the towns, meant increased prosperity for those who remained on the land.

Horticulture, meanwhile, remained the province of the wealthy. The average farmer had little interest in anything outside his crops; it was his wife who inherited a long tradition of kitchen and flower gardening. The practice of using female – and even child – labor in the fields meant that few wives of the poorer farmers and farm laborers had any time or energy left to cultivate their own gardens. Similarly, city women worked equally long and exhausting hours in the factories, so the skills of cultivation and preservation were forgotten.

Among the better off families, vegetable and herb gardens flourished as they had for centuries,

THRESHING, 1860

providing most of the food for the household. On a typical farm the diet often did not extend much beyond cabbages, beans and potatoes, to accompany the regular roasts of bacon, beef and occasionally mutton; apples, pears and soft fruit in season and some herbs for flavor and medicinal use. Of course the farmer's wife had also to make her own butter and cheese, look after her poultry, and bake her bread, apart from preserving her fruits, cleaning her house, making and mending most of her family's clothes and, frequently, teaching her children, so she hardly had much time left to devote to raising exotic blooms.

In the gardens of the great estates, however, not only were all the standard fruits and vegetables grown for the use of the family, but fig, vine and melon houses were also built. Peach, plum and nectarine trees lined the protected walls of kitchen gardens, and orchids and tropical lilies were raised in heated and carefully ventilated greenhouses. Sometimes as many as fifty gardeners were employed on these estates but they produced a range of fruit and vegetables scarcely equalled until the arrival of refrigerated airfreight.

Similar sized commercial market gardens flourished on the outskirts of all the larger towns and cities. Although the development of the railroad system meant that produce could be transported much more quickly from far afield, there was still a huge market for locally grown fruit and vegetables. The smallholdings grew anything from cabbages or cauliflowers to soft fruits. The produce was taken daily to the towns to be sold either direct to the public or wholesale to the established shops and market stalls.

CHAPTER TEN

FOOD FROM THE STREET STALLS OF LONDON

In 1849 a series of articles appeared in the *Morning Chronicle* that were to shock and horrify the paper's middle class readers, and that were to be published two years later, in three large volumes called *London Labour and London Poor*. Their author was Henry Mayhew, an impecunious journalist and writer. He came from a good middle class family (his father was a lawyer), and was educated at Westminster, from which school he ran away to India. On his return he studied law, but the law seemed dull beside the lure of journalism and was soon abandoned. From 1831-39 he ran a satirical weekly magazine called *Figaro* in London; in 1841 he co-founded *Punch* although his association with the magazine was to be short. By that time he had become involved in his mammoth investigation into the murky world of London's poor, a world that came to fascinate him and that he was to explore with unflagging energy for over twenty years.

The portrait of Mayhew that appears in the front of his trilogy shows him as a portly and slightly self-important Victorian, yet friends' comments suggest a far more likeable and entertaining character. Charm he must certainly have had to be able to penetrate the lowest dives in the slums of London safely and to persuade his poor, hungry, fearful, illiterate and often resentful subjects to pour out their hearts and souls to him. The result of his years of labor is a fascinating picture of London's poor that has not faded with the years.

Mayhew's descriptions are remarkable in both

their detail and their compassionately objective approach. The scenes that he describes are quite as horrific as anything that appear in Dickens, yet they are free from the novelist's melodramatic touch. In each piece, the man, woman or child he is interviewing is allowed to speak for himself or herself, his or her words being recorded with total fidelity and a wonderful ear for colloquialism and accent.

The majority of Mayhew's interviewees earned their livings on the streets selling commodities, including a great deal of food and drink, either to each other or to the better off citizens in London's West End. Mayhew estimated that there were about thirty-five thousand people living off street trading in London in the 1840s and 1850s. Of these the most successful, and the largest contingent, were those who had been born to the streets. Then there were the working, often skilled, men and women who had been forced on to the streets because they had lost their jobs or, in the case of the women, the family breadwinners. The Irish potato famine of 1848 and the cholera epidemic of 1848-49 brought a great new wave of poor, both English and Irish, into the already overcrowded slums of the East End. These newcomers were not usually very successful; they did not know the ways of the streets, were easily gulled or swindled and had little skill in hawking their wares.

Street trading was a precarious business at the best of times and the traders, or "costermongers," were an improvident lot. When times were good they put little by out of the average of ten shillings per week that Mayhew reckoned they earned, so that a dose of bad weather, which kept their customers off the streets, could "reduce them to starvation within three days." Nonethe-

OPPOSITE: MUSSEL SAUSAGES AND PEASE SOUP

— *123* —

less, when times were good they enjoyed them-selves, in the many taverns and beer shops where they drank and played cards and shove-half-penny or skittles, usually to the detriment of their pockets, or in theaters and music halls such as the Coburg or "Vic" (now the Old Vic) where "love and murder" were the most popular sub-jects!

Street trading of food fell into the raw and the cooked categories. Uncooked fruits, vegetables, meats, fishes and so on were sold mainly to the better-off classes whose cooks would prepare them for the table. The costers themselves, since they were on the streets from dawn till long after dusk, ate mainly "in the street" – "an outdoor diet" as Mayhew calls it. He continues: "They breakfast at a coffee stall. For a penny they can procure a small cup of coffee and two 'thin' (that is to say two thin slices of bread and butter). For dinner, which is hardly ever eaten at the costermonger's abode, they buy 'block orna-ments' as they call them: small dark colored pieces of meat exposed on the cheap butchers" blocks. These they cook in a tap room; half a pound costing 2d. If time be an object the coster buys a hot pie or two, preferring fruit pies when in season, and next to them, meat pies. Saveloys with a pint of beer or a glass of 'short' (neat gin) is with them another common weekday dinner. The costers make all possible purchases of the street dealers and pride themselves on thus 'sticking to their own.'"

In the costers' language, the ready prepared food fell into four categories: "solids," pastries, "sweetstuffs" and "drinkables." The "solids" included hot eels, pickled whelks, oysters, sheep's trotters, pea soup, fried fish, ham sand-wiches, hot green peas, kidney and boiled meat puddings, beef, mutton, kidney and eel pies and baked potatoes. The pastries "which tempt the street eaters are tarts of rhubarb, currant, goose-berry, cherry, apples, damson, cranberry and mincemeat; plum dough and plum cake; lard, currant, almond and many other varieties of cakes; Chelsea buns; gingerbread nuts; muffins and crumpets." The "sweetstuffs" included "several kinds of rock, sticks, lozenges, hard-bakes and cough drops and lastly, the more novel and aristocratic luxury of street ices and straw-berry cream at 1d a glass." The "drinkables" were tea, coffee and cocoa; ginger beer, lemon-ade, Persian sherbet; hot elder cordial or wine;

peppermint water; curds and whey; water (as at Hampstead); rice milk and milk in the parks, where cows were still kept and could be milked for a penny a pint.

WATERCRESS AND POTATO SOUP

Serves 10

Among the poorest of the costermongers were the women and children who carried "creases," or watercress, bought in Farringdon market, through the streets in large wicker baskets and sold it for "four bunches a penny."

INGREDIENTS

3 large bunches watercress, fairly finely chopped
¼ lb potatoes, scrubbed and thickly sliced
3 tablespoons red or white wine vinegar
2 teaspoons salt
2½ quarts water
salt and freshly ground black pepper

Put all the ingredients in a large pan, bring to a boil and simmer for 30 to 45 minutes, or until the potatoes are completely cooked. They should completely disintegrate, in which case you can serve the soup as it is. If not, you will need to blend the soup roughly in a food processor. Sea-son to taste with more salt and pepper and serve with large hunks of bread.

A CHEAP PEASE SOUP

Serves 10

Pea soup, hot "peascods" and pease pudding were all popular street dishes, made sometimes from fresh peas but usually from dried or split ones. When the fogs caused by thousands of coal fires were really bad, they were called "peasoupers" because they were as thick and yellowy green as a bowl of good pea soup. This particular recipe comes from Soyer's *Shilling Cookery*.

INGREDIENTS

2 tablespoons lard or bacon fat
2 oz diced bacon
1 large onion, sliced
2 medium turnips, diced
2 medium carrots, diced
1 leek, cleaned and sliced
3 celery stalks, chopped
2½ quarts water
1¼ cups yellow split peas
about 1 teaspoon salt
1 heaped teaspoon sugar
1 heaped teaspoon dried mint
½ cup all-purpose flour (optional)

Heat the fat in a large, heavy pan and fry the bacon and onion briskly until it is well browned but not burned. Add the turnips, carrots, leek and celery and fry for a further 10 minutes. Add the water and the split peas, bring to a boil and simmer gently for 2 to 3 hours, or until the peas are quite pulped. At this stage you can purée the soup if you would like a smoother texture. Add the salt, sugar and mint, and thicken the soup, if necessary, with the flour worked to a paste with ¾ cup of water. Adjust the seasoning to taste and serve the soup with lots of fresh, crusty bread.

OYSTER OR MUSSEL SAUSAGES

Serves 10

Even a hundred and fifty years ago oysters were too expensive for the very poor; they were sold mainly to working and trades people, and gentlemen "down on their luck," who ate them heavily dosed with pepper. Any that were left at the end of the day might have been turned into sausages for home consumption as they would probably not have been saleable the next day. Today oysters are so expensive that I have substituted the cheaper alternative mussels.

INGREDIENTS

1½ lb mussels (frozen ones will do very
 well)
4¼ cups brown bread crumbs
1¼ cups ground beef suet or shortening
1 teaspoon salt
1 teaspoon mace
1 teaspoon nutmeg
½ teaspoon cayenne
3 eggs
seasoned whole-wheat flour
butter or oil for frying

Grind the mussels coarsely in a food processor or blender, or chop them by hand. Mix them with the bread crumbs and suet, then mix in the salt and spices thoroughly. Beat the eggs with a fork and stir them into the sausage mixture. Use your fingers to make sausage or cake shapes and roll them in the flour. Fry them gently in the butter or oil until they are well browned on all sides – about 5 minutes – and drain them for a minute or two on paper towels before serving. The sausages will reheat well and also taste very good cold.

STUFFED OX HEART AND LIVER

Serves 10

Although the costermongers ate most of their meals "in the streets," Sunday was the one day, provided the week's takings had been good, on which they would have a proper dinner at home. This might be a roast and "taters," or, if the money had not been quite so good, a stew made from the cheaper hearts and livers. The recipe is from Alexis Soyer's *Shilling Cookery* book.

INGREDIENTS

½ lb ox liver, finely chopped
3 slices of bacon, chopped
1 small onion, finely chopped
¼ cup ground beef suet
6 fresh sage leaves, chopped, or 2
  teaspoons dried
salt and black pepper
1 whole ox heart (about 2¼ lb), cleaned
3 medium onions
1¾ cups navy beans, soaked in cold
  water for 2 hours
2½ quarts water

Mix the liver, bacon, onions, suet and sage well and season it generously. Open up the heart as much as possible and fill it with the stuffing. Either tie it back into shape with string or wrap it in cheesecloth. Put it into a moderately large pan with the whole onions and navy beans. Add the water, 1 teaspoon salt and plenty of black pepper. Cover, bring to a boil and simmer for 3 to 4 hours. You could also cook the heart in a slow cookpot overnight. Strain off the cooking liquid, cool it entirely and remove the fat. Pour as much as seems reasonable back into the pot with the heart and reheat it in the juices. To serve, untie the heart from its string or cloth and put it in a warmed serving dish surrounded by the onions and navy beans. Pour the juice around and serve immediately with mashed or boiled potatoes.

HOT EEL PIE

Serves 10

Hot pies were always popular with the street people, although one man reported to Mayhew that they never "ate eel pies because we know they're often made of large dead eels. *We*, of all people, are not to be 'ad that way. But the haristocrats eats 'em and never knows the difference." Street pies would probably have been made of suet pastry and boiled (like the Beefsteak Pudding on page 113). This recipe, however, is for a somewhat lighter pie and comes from Kettner's *Book of the Table* – the pastry is Dr. Kitchiner's. It should be made with fresh eels but if you have difficulty getting them, jellied eel will do very well instead.

INGREDIENTS

about 2 lb small eel, cut in pieces
4 shallots, finely chopped
3 bouquets garnis
salt and pepper
generous pinch of nutmeg
1¼ cups medium sherry
4 tablespoons butter
½ cup whole-wheat flour
juice of 1 lemon
4 hard-cooked eggs

Put the eels into a pan with the shallots, bouquets garnis, seasoning, sherry and enough water to cover them. Bring to a boil, simmer for 2 minutes only, then remove the pieces with a perforated spoon and arrange them in a large pie dish interspersed with the sliced hard-cooked eggs. If the eel mixture does not come very high up in the dish, use a pie support for the pastry. If you are using jellied eel, heat the pieces gently with their jelly, the shallots, bouquets garnis and seasoning just to boiling point. Transfer the eels immediately to the pie dish as above.

Mix the butter with the flour to make a smooth paste, then add 3¾ cups of the cooking liquid slowly. Return to the pan, bring to a boil and cook gently to thicken. Season to taste with salt, pepper and lemon juice and pour this juice over the eel mixture in the pie dish. Cover with puff pastry (opposite) and bake at 375° for 25 minutes, or until the pastry is puffed and lightly browned. Serve hot or warm.

STUFFED OX HEART AND LIVER AND HOT EEL PIE

PUFF PASTRY

INGREDIENTS

*2 sticks plus 6 tablespoons butter
3 cups whole-wheat flour, well sifted
2/3 cup water*

Rub 1 stick plus 2 tablespoons of the butter into the flour gently and mix to a stiff paste with the water. Knead it well for a few minutes, then set it aside in a cool place for 30 minutes. Roll the paste out as thinly as you can. Cut up the remaining butter in little pieces and sprinkle these over the paste. To quote Dr. Kitchiner: "Throw on a little flour, double the paste up in folds and roll it out thin three times, then set aside for about an hour *in a cold place.*" Roll the paste out and cover the eel pie (opposite) in the normal way.

SHEEPS' OR PIGS' FEET

Serves 10

Sheeps' feet are seldom seen these days and pigs' ones are only used to give a gelatinous quality to a stew or casserole but in Victorian London they were very popular, mainly because of their cheapness. They are certainly not over-endowed with meat, but the cooking juices in which they are served make up for the overdose of bones. This recipe comes from Francatelli's *Plain Cookery Book for the Working Classes*.

INGREDIENTS

10 sheeps' or pigs' feet, well cleaned
5 cups milk
5 cups water
2 teaspoons salt
3 teaspoons fresh or 2 teaspoons dried thyme
handful of peppercorns
⅔ cup white wine vinegar
4 tablespoons butter
½ cup all-purpose flour
6 large handfuls of fresh parsley, chopped

Put the feet into a large pan with the milk, water, salt, thyme, peppercorns and vinegar. Bring to a boil slowly and simmer gently for at least 3 hours. Remove the feet with a perforated spoon, and boil the juices briskly until they are reduced to about 5 cups. Allow the sauce to cool completely, then skim any excess fat from the top. Reheat the sauce gently. Mix the butter thoroughly with the flour in a small bowl, add some of the hot sauce to make a smooth paste, then return it all to the sauce. Cook for a few minutes for the sauce to thicken. Add the feet to reheat gently in the sauce. Finally, add the parsley and adjust the seasoning to taste. Serve in bowls with lots of sauce and plenty of brown bread and butter.

BAKED POTATOES

"The *baked potato trade*, in the way it is at present carried on, has not been known more than fifteen years in the streets . . . There are usually from 280 to 300 potatoes in the hundredweight; these are cleaned by the huckster and, when dried, taken in baskets to the bakers to be cooked. They are baked in tins, and require an hour and a half to do them well. The charge for baking is 9d the hundredweight. They are taken home from the bakehouse in baskets, with a yard and a half of green baize in which they are covered up and so protected from the cold. The huckster then places them in his can, which consists of a tin, with a half lid; it stands on four legs, and has a large handle to it, with an iron fire pot suspended immediately beneath the vessel which is used for holding the potatoes. Directly over the firepot is a boiler for hot water. This is concealed within the vessel and serves to keep the potatoes always hot. Outside the vessel where the potatoes are kept is, at one end a small com-

THE BAKED POTATO MAN.

partment for butter and salt, and at the other end another compartment for fresh charcoal. Above the boiler and beside the lid is a small pipe for carrying off the steam. These potato cans are sometimes brightly polished, sometimes painted red and occasionally brass mounted. The baked potato man usually devotes half an hour to polishing them up and they are mostly kept as bright as silver."

Bake your potatoes in the usual way and serve with lots of butter and salt. Alexis Soyer, in his *Shilling Cookery,* also suggests par-cooking the potatoes, then partially hollowing them out and filling them with sausage meat. Return them to the oven and finish baking as normal.

PLUM DUFF OR DOUGH
Serves 10

"Plum dough is one of the street-eatables – though perhaps it is rather a violence to class it with the street pastry – which is usually made by the vendors. It is simply a boiled plum or currant pudding of the plainest description . . . The puddings are boiled in cotton bags, in coppers or large pans; the charge is a half-penny each."

The "duff" is certainly designed to warm the cockles of the heart and keep out the winter cold and although the street ones may have been a bit basic, with an extra handful or two of currants, a plum duff can be very tasty. The original recipe came from Francatelli's *Plain Cookery Book for the Working Classes.*

INGREDIENTS

*4 teaspoons raw cane sugar
1 tablespoon dry yeast or 1 cake
    compressed yeast
about 1¼ cups warm water
2 cups whole-wheat flour
1 teaspoon salt
⅔ cup raisins
1 teaspoon allspice
milk*

Put a teaspoon of the sugar with the yeast in a small bowl and add a little of the water. Stir to a cream and leave for a few minutes to froth. Make a well in the flour, pour in the yeast mixture and the remaining water and mix to a stiff dough. Set aside, covered, in a warmish place and leave to rise for 1½ to 2 hours. Punch the dough down and add the raisins, the remaining sugar, the allspice and a little milk to make a slightly softer dough; knead for a few minutes.

You can then make one big "duff" or dumpling, or several smaller ones. In either case, tie up the dough loosely in a cloth and lower it into a pot of fast boiling water. Cover and boil briskly for 1 to 1½ hours depending on the size of the duffs. Remove from the water, drain and then remove the cloth. Serve as soon as possible either by themselves or with a rich custard (page 116).

GINGERBREAD
Makes 16 to 20 pieces

Gingerbread and ginger nuts were great favorites on the London streets. The costermongers bought them, with most of the other cakes and biscuits, none of which they made themselves, from the Jewish pastry cooks who lived around Whitechapel. They then sold them in the parks and at the fairs. This recipe comes from Dr. Kitchiner's *Cook's Oracle* and makes a strong, rich, deliciously gooey bread.

INGREDIENTS

*2 cups whole-wheat flour
⅓ cup candied orange or lemon or
    mixed peel
⅔ cup raw cane sugar
2 heaped teaspoons ginger
1 heaped teaspoon allspice
⅓ cup molasses
1 stick butter*

Mix the flour with the candied peel, sugar, ginger and allspice in a bowl. Meanwhile heat the molasses with the butter until both are malleable, then work them into the dry ingredients. Press the mixture into an 8 inch round or square baking pan and bake at 325° for 25 minutes. Remove and cut into biscuit shapes before the gingerbread cools. When it has cooled slightly, remove it on to a rack.

MUFFINS
Makes 10 to 15 muffins

Muffins were bought early in the morning from the bakers, wrapped in a cloth to keep them warm, then layered in a wicker tray that was carried on the head. The muffins were mainly hawked in the more affluent squares and crescents where many a household would waken to the sound of the muffin man's bell. The original muffins would have been made with fresh yeast or ale barm but using dry makes the business a good deal simpler.

INGREDIENTS

1 tablespoon dry yeast or 1 cake
*   compressed yeast*
½ teaspoon sugar
1¼ cups milk, just warmer than your
*   finger*
4 cups whole-wheat flour
2 eggs, beaten
2 tablespoons butter or margarine
oil or butter for cooking

Mix the yeast with the sugar and a little of the warm milk and leave to froth. Then mix in all the other ingredients. Knead the dough for 5 minutes, then cut into about fifteen pieces. Knead each one, shape it into a ball, place it on a warmed, oiled baking sheet or piece of foil and flatten it slightly. Brush the top with oil and leave to rise for 30 minutes at room temperature. Heat a griddle and brush lightly with oil – if you don't have a griddle, a heavy frying pan will do. Cook the muffins for about 5 minutes on each side, reducing the heat slightly after the first minute. Eat warm with butter.

GINGERBREAD (TOP LEFT), MUFFINS (TOP RIGHT) AND PLUM DUFF WITH CUSTARD

SHOPS AND MARKETS

LEADENHALL MARKET IN 1845

It was not until the second half of the 19th century that shops began to assume a form that a modern shopper would recognize. Until then there were no food shops, as we know them, selling perishable and nonperishable foods on a daily basis. In the country, many households were still largely self-sufficient, at least as far as the most basic foodstuffs were concerned; the villages and towns relied on local daily or weekly markets and periodic fairs to supply their needs.

Bigger towns and cities such as Liverpool acknowledged the needs of their growing populations by building decorative covered arcades to accommodate the regular market traders, Leadenhall Market in London is another example. But the majority of business was done in the often chaotic outdoor markets, set up in small alleys or open streets. The market traders were divided between those who brought their own farm or dairy produce to sell, and those who were simply retailers, buying their goods in the wholesale markets. Even in the larger towns a surprising amount of food was brought in daily from the surrounding countryside.

Whatever was not sold on the stalls could be obtained from the individual hawkers who tramped the streets of poor and better class districts alike, selling anything from butcher's meat, milk and muffins to boot blacking, ribbons and laces. Another version of the hawker was the cheap jack or journeyman who, with his horse and cart, bought up his stock and traveled the country markets, fairs and big houses. He was a relative aristocrat among traders as it was reckoned that he needed one hundred pounds' worth of stock, apart from his horse and cart, to be successful. He sold mainly hardware items, but was not above picking up, and passing on, a good bargain wherever he found one.

There were of course shops too, to deal with the innumerable goods other than food needed to keep a community going. At the beginning of the century these were mainly small, owner-run shops, specializing in their particular trade. To a large extent such specialization was still necessary since the shopkeeper often had to "finish" the articles he was to sell. Butchers had to buy their meat "on the hoof" so they had to know how to slaughter and dress it for sale; grocers had to understand how to choose, blend and package much of their stock and even haberdashers bought their cotton and silk by weight and had to cut and fold it into lengths for sale. So, shops remained small, their owners skilled craftsmen and their assistants "apprentices" who lived above the shop with the family and learned their trade. Among such smaller shops were those selling goods or services manufactured or provided on the premises. These might include tailors, shoemakers, milliners, bakers, coal or timber merchants, barbers, joiners, blacksmiths and maybe a boiled sweet maker – apart of course from several beer shops. For example, Aldeburgh, a small Suffolk village with a population of thirteen hundred in the 1830s "held markets on Wednesdays and Saturdays, fairs in March and May, and boasted eight inns or public houses, six shoemakers (leather shoes wore out much faster when there was no public transport), four grocer-cum-drapers, two haberdashers, three bakers, two chemists, four tailors, three milliners, five blacksmiths, a saddler, a coachmaker, a hairdresser and a carrier two days a week to nearby Ipswich." Of course in many cases, especially in smaller towns, the grocer or the draper would in effect become a "general store."

The two trades that made some movement

toward retailing on a larger scale were haberdashery and drapery. This was possible because their goods had been among the first to be mechanized so a wider range of finished, cheaper goods could be supplied. Such shops grew closer to 20th century proportions, many of them combining their retailing business with wholesaling of their goods to other smaller merchants, journeymen or shopkeepers. Assistants in drapers' and haberdashers' shops also "lived in," but they fared far worse than those in the smaller shops, where the two or three assistants were usually treated as "family." In the early part of the century, drapers' assistants were nearly all young men, although women had gained a substantial foothold by the 1880s. The work was hard, the hours very long (up at 6 am to clean a shop which would not close till 10 pm), the pay paltry and the living conditions cramped and uncomfortable – and Sundays were their only free day.

Many of these shops dealt to a large extent on credit. This situation arose both from a general shortage of "small change" and from the difficulty that the new wage-earners had in managing their meager salaries. The system was chaotic and inefficient, and opened the way to appalling corruption and swindling on the part of the shopkeepers. Many not only extorted fifty to a hundred percent interest but also charged more initially for their goods to cover the credit service. The result was that families' weekly wages were often totally consumed by the previous week's debts. Alternatively, the family's possessions spent much of every week at the pawn shop, being retrieved each Saturday, only to find their way back by the following Monday or Tuesday. Well-organized families paid with ready cash and got better value.

As the 19th century progressed, the population, especially in the cities, grew rapidly and, almost imperceptibly, the general standard of living rose. The result was two major developments affecting retail shopping. One was the introduction of the "co-op" and "chain store." The "co-operative" stores were particularly successful in the north of England. The theory was that customers paid a decent cash price for their goods but thereby acquired a stake in the business. Provided trade was good, they could expect a return, in the form of a "divi" or dividend, every six months or year. The success of the co-

ops in the second half of the century was partly due to the fact that the main shops opened smaller branches for the convenience of their outlying customers – a practice that had previously been considered unprofitable, but which turned out to be quite the opposite. The co-operative movement also found it more convenient for a central agent to buy goods for a number of stores, thus getting the best buys at the best prices and the financial rewards of buying in bulk.

The second development arose through the enormous increase in cheap transport from the 1850s onward, both in Britain and overseas. Basic foodstuffs could now be imported cheaply, prepared and packed at a central warehouse and delivered, ready to sell, to as many outlets as were available. Bottled jams, pickles and sauces, packets of custard powder and gravy powder and canned goods were soon available too. The outlets could be basic and the staff needed no special skills or training, so costs, and therefore prices, could be kept low. Thomas Lipton opened the first of these shops in Glasgow in 1872; twenty-six years later he had two hundred and forty-five branches all over the country. The formula was so successful that the old-style grocers were forced to change their ways, and 20th century shopping was born.

Transporting farm products to town, 1898

E D W A R D A B B O T T ,
A U S T R A L I A N
A R I S T O L O G I S T

Unlike any other country in the "western" world, Australia had no tradition of indigenous peasantry tilling the land and living off its fruits on which to base its gastronomic development. The aborigines, who had roamed the deserts for forty thousand years before the arrival of Captain Cook, were hunters, killing whatever animals came their way; they made no attempt to cultivate the land.

The original colonists who arrived in 1788 were mostly town-bred, from the lowest levels of society where training in husbandry or housekeeping was nonexistent, and totally anglophile in their outlook. They had brought enough rations to allow them to survive for a couple of years, on the assumption that they would then be able to grow much of their own food. However, the availability of weekly rations – 7 pounds flour, 7 pounds beef or pork, 7½ cups dried peas, ⅔ cup butter and 1 cup rice per adult, if they were lucky – and the difficulty the colonists had in establishing familiar crops severely hampered any chance of developing a "native" cuisine.

The situation was exacerbated by the discovery that fortunes could be made from grazing sheep on Australia's vast hinterland. The few shepherds needed to care for them were easy to recruit from the large population of ex-convicts who squatted on the land outside the main settlements. The shepherds were paid in rations, supplemented by just enough cash to buy just enough drink to get roaring drunk on each pay day. Their rations consisted of 10 pounds flour, 10 pounds meat (salted pork, corned beef or newly killed mutton), 2 pounds sugar, ¼ lb tea and salt per week.

OPPOSITE: SHELLFISH SALAD

Such prodigality with meat spelled riches to poor Europeans, but in every other respect the rations were a disaster: the flour was baked, unleavened on a stone into the famous "damper;" the meat was boiled or roasted in the fire; the tea was boiled long and hard with the sugar. Not only was no art required to prepare such food and little pleasure derived from eating it, but everything except the mutton had to be imported. On these men and their way of life was the legend of Australia – and her food – built.

Of course, that is not the whole story. The coastal settlements were much more successful in establishing some sort of agriculture. The "Dungaree" settlers along the Hawkesbury valley, for example, grew grain, fruits and vegetables that they sold in the town markets, and later in the 19th century, the Chinese who came in their thousands to seek gold, ran flourishing market gardens – but the vast majority of the settlers preferred to buy their food ready made. As Louisa Anne Meredith, arriving in 1839 as the bride of a successful squatter, noted in her diary: "[For the average settler] nothing demanding bodily exertion is attempted. Meat can run about and feed itself on the wild hills, and flour they can buy; fruit and vegetables they 'don't heed,' as they would demand some little labour to produce."

It is hardly surprising that Australian cooking reduced a Frenchman, Edmond Marin La Meslée, visiting the country in the 1840s, to complain that:
"It is true to say that no other country on earth offers more of everything needed to make a good meal, or offers it more cheaply, than Australia; but there is no other country either where the cuisine is more elementary, not to say abominable."

However, across the water in Tasmania, then known as Van Dieman's Land, the climate was milder, the soil fertile, and the settlers more willing to use the indigenous foods. Within twelve years of the colony's foundation it was exporting food to the mainland and by 1851 Henry Melville, in *The Present State of Australia,* was waxing lyrical about the fruits, the wonderful potatoes, the bees – and the beauty of the ladies' complexions . . .

An important person in this flourishing colony was one Edward Abbott whose father had become deputy-judge-advocate in Hobart in 1815. Abbott himself was well educated, wealthy, well traveled – and fascinated by food. In 1864 he published *The English and Australian Cook Book. Cookery for the many as well as for the Upper Ten Thousand – by an Australian Aristologist* (a student of the art of dining). It was the first, and indeed only, serious cook book to be published in Australia in the first hundred years of its existence. In his preface Abbott declares: "I am desirous of some reform in the *cuisine* of some of my countrymen's establishments, and I am vain enough to believe that I shall effect that object by this publication – one which would combine 'the advantages of Mrs. Acton's work with the *crème de la crème* of the cheapest of Soyer's productions.'" Alas, his countrymen were unresponsive and *The English and Australian Cook Book* never reached a second edition.

The Aristologist's book deserved better. In its one hundred and three bewildering chapters it covers everything from the standard soups and sauces to Dinner Party Precedence, Old Tusser's Good and Bad Housewifery, Magical drinks, German sour-krout (*sic*), Cookery for the Destitute, Pyroligneous acid, Hebrew Refections, and a chapter on Why Animals to be Eaten must be Killed. Like the Beetons, working at exactly the same time back in England, Abbott also crammed his book with comments, aphorisms, medical information and snippets of natural history. Nor was he hesitant in propounding his own theories:
"SUPPERS AND LUNCHEONS We say little respecting the above, because we consider them unnecessary and unwholesome. A person who partakes of luncheon cannot possibly enjoy his dinner; and anyone eating supper must loathe his breakfast, which ought to be the principal meal of the day."

Abbott's recipes have been culled not only from Mrs. Acton and Soyer but from Izaac Walton, Yarrell's *British Fishes,* the Hop Pole in Worcester, the *Scientific American* and countless equally diverse sources, including the many friends who contributed most of the quite large section on cooking the native species: kangaroo, emu, wombat, canvas back ducks and so on. Abbott gives no less than ten recipes for kangaroo; to give some feel of the Aristologist's style here is his own recipe for Kangaroo Steamer – with addenda:
"This is a simple species of braise, and, as its name imports, the meat is steamed. Cut the meat in pieces of about a quarter of an inch square, and put it into a pan with a well covered lid, with a spoonful of milk, an onion shredded into small pieces, and some pepper and salt to taste. When it has been on the fire a short time add about a tenth in quantity of salt pork, of bacon cut to the same size as the kangaroo, with a spoonful of ketchup. Serve hot, with jelly."

"No one can tell what a steamer is unless it has been tasted; indeed it affords an excellent repast; and it is surprising that the steamer, preserved in tins, has not yet been exported to England."
The Present State of Australia, Henry Melville.

"KANGAROO Usually mild, inoffensive animals, they are sometimes stirred up to wrath when brought to bay by dogs; and there are two instances on record of 'boomers' (forest Kangaroos) having seized men in their arms and carried them some distance and then thrown them violently down. I have seen the haunches of a boomer which weighed ninety six pounds and stood seven feet high."
Mr. Hull.

I have tried to choose a wide selection of Abbott's dishes, allowing him, wherever possible, to introduce his own recipes.

SOUP A LA MOUSQUETAIRE
Serves 6

The following quotation appears with reference to nothing in particular at the end of the chapter on Made Dishes – but seems to be more pertinent at the beginning of the meal:

"THIRTEEN TO DINNER   There is a prejudice generally in the pretended danger of being thirteen to the table. If the probability be required, that out of the thirteen persons of different ages one of them at least shall die within a year, it will be found that the chances are about ten to one, that one death at least will occur. This calculation, by means of false interpretation, has given rise to the prejudice, no less ridiculous, that the danger will be avoided by inviting a greater number of guests, which can only have the effect of augmenting the probability of the event so much apprehended. *Quetelet, on the Calculation of Probabilities.*"

I would hope that the guests managed to get some Soup à la Mousequetaire down before Nemesis caught up with them! Incidentally, this is an excellent way to use up the remains of a roast of lamb or mutton.

INGREDIENTS

2 cups fresh or frozen green peas
3 cups roughly chopped, fresh spinach
   or sorrel
1 cup roughly chopped, cooked
   (preferably roast) lamb or mutton
the cooked lamb or mutton bone if
   available
1¼ cups dry white wine
5 cups water
salt and pepper

Put the peas and spinach or sorrel in a pan large enough to hold the meat bone if you have one. Then add the lamb or mutton, with its bone, the wine and water. Bring to the boil and simmer for 1 hour. Remove the bone and blend the soup in a food processor, then rub it through a strainer – you will have a lot of debris left but that does not matter. Discard the debris, return the soup to the pan, reheat it and season to taste with salt and pepper. Serve hot. You can add a dollop of lightly whipped cream to each serving if you want, but I do not think it is necessary.

SHELLFISH SALAD
Serves 6

Despite the Aristologist's enthusiasm for salads and their digestibility (see page 140) he is surprisingly reticent about fish, usually thought of as the most digestible of foods. Indeed, in his chapter on "Digestion" only oysters are given a "digestion timetable:" 2 hours and 30 minutes for raw ones, 3 hours and 30 minutes for stewed ones. To be on the safe side one should probably allow as long for other shellfish. The original recipe calls for lobster and crayfish but the salad works equally well with less exotic shellfish in case you are not feeling that extravagant.

INGREDIENTS

1 lb potatoes
6 hard-cooked egg yolks
4 tablespoons white wine vinegar
8 tablespoons olive oil
4 teaspoons wholegrain or French
   mustard
1 teaspoon salt
½ teaspoon cayenne
about 4 tablespoons milk or light cream
1½ lb cooked shellfish, cut into fairly
   small pieces – about ¾ inch
1–2 crisp lettuce hearts, roughly
   chopped
watercress, parsley or slices of lemon to
   garnish

Scrub and boil or steam the potatoes in their skins. Cool them slightly, then skin them and mash with the hard-cooked egg yolks. Add the vinegar, oil, salt and cayenne, then reduce the purée with the milk or cream. When it is really well amalgamated, mix in the shellfish and adjust the seasoning to taste. Allow to cool completely.

Make a bed of the lettuce on a serving dish. Pile the potato and fish mixture in the middle and garnish with some watercress, parsley, or a few lemon twists, before serving.

ROAST LEG OF MUTTON OR LAMB WITH GARLIC
Serves 6

"Being at Bordeaux, we one day gave a dinner, at the hotel at which we lodged, to a few English friends whom we had met there. Anxious to taste, and let our guests taste, a _gigot à l'ail_, a dish for which the Bordelais cooks are celebrated, we ordered one as part of the repast. When the roast was placed on the table at the second course, it appeared to us all to be a _gigot aux haricots;_ but the meat was delicious and the beans were certainly superior to, and bearing a different flavour from, any _haricots_ we had ever tasted before. Vexed, however, at what we considered an in-attention to our orders, we summoned the landlord, and begged to know why, when we had ordered a _gigot à l'ail_ he had presumed to send up a _gigot aux haricots_. 'I have shown no inattention,' he replied, 'and made no mistake. The dish which you have just eaten, and which your guests seemed to have liked, was a _gigot à l'ail_, and what you have mistaken for beans is garlic.'

"'Is it possible!' we exclaimed. Again we tasted the garlic; its rankness was gone; but there was in it a delicious flavour for which we could not account. After apologising to our host, 'If the question be not indiscreet, and the matter no secret, how can you impart this delicious flavour to garlic?' we asked. 'There is no secret in the case,' he replied; 'the process is very simple. The garlic is thrown into five boiling waters, with a little salt, and boiled five minutes in each. It is then drained and put into the dripping pan under the roasting mutton.'"

Maybe garlic has mellowed over the last hundred years, but I found that three boilings were really enough as with five the cloves started to disintegrate. If you can get a small leg of mutton, do use it; if not, lamb is equally good.

INGREDIENTS

1 small leg of mutton or medium leg of
_ lamb – about 4½ lb_
12 garlic heads
salt
1 tablespoon whole-wheat flour
about ⅔ cup red wine
pinch of dark brown sugar

Peel all the garlic heads – this is a longish business but there is no way round it. Put the cloves into a pan, cover with lightly salted boiling water and boil for 5 minutes. Repeat this process twice more, then drain the cloves thoroughly. Spread them over the bottom of a baking pan, but keep them close enough together to remain under the meat or they will dry up and burn. Place the leg of mutton or lamb on a baking rack over the garlic. Roast for 20 minutes per pound, or a little longer if you are using mutton. When the meat is cooked, remove it on to a warmed serving dish. Remove the garlic cloves with a perforated spoon and pile them around the meat – keep both warm.

Drain any excess fat from the pan, then add the flour, stir and cook over a gentle heat for a few minutes. Gradually add red wine and enough water to thin the sauce to gravy consistency. Season to taste with salt, pepper and a little dark brown sugar. Serve with the lamb or mutton. Boiled or steamed new potatoes and any green vegetable are excellent with it.

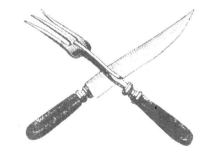

ROAST OX TONGUE
Serves 6

"This is a very good dish," says Mr. Abbott, and indeed it is. I was a little nervous about only roasting the tongue as I feared it might be tough, so I took the liberty of adapting the recipe to allow for a couple of hours of boiling before it went into the oven.

INGREDIENTS

1 fresh ox tongue, about 3 lb
6 cloves
½ teaspoon salt
thinly peeled rind of 1 lemon
⅔ cup port
2 tablespoons butter

ROAST LEG OF LAMB WITH GARLIC (LEFT)
AND ROAST OX TONGUE

Wash the tongue thoroughly and trim any bits of root that may be left. Put into a saucepan just big enough to hold it with the cloves, salt, lemon rind and port and just cover with water. Bring to a boil and simmer gently for 2 hours. Remove the tongue carefully from the pan, allow it to cool slightly, then skin it and place it in a roasting pan. Melt the butter and brush the tongue thoroughly with it. Roast at 350° for 45 minutes, basting every now and then with the butter.

Meanwhile, strain the cooking juices and return them to the pan. Boil them fairly briskly for 15 to 20 minutes, or until they are substantially reduced. Season to taste.

Serve the tongue on a bed of watercress or green vegetable such as spinach, accompanied by the sauce. The tongue is also excellent cold.

VEAL EN PAPILLOTE

Serves 6

This recipe comes from the chapter on Frying and is headed by some odd remarks:
"Under an impoverished diet, the moral and intellectial capacity is deteriorated, as well as the bodily." Coombe.
"NOT GENERALLY KNOWN. I have learned by experience that of all the fats that are used for frying, the pot top, which is taken from the surface of the broth and stock pot, is far the best." *L'Art de Cuisinier.*

In fact, I decided to bake the *papillotes,* as they would not fit easily into a frying pan, but the result is much the same.

INGREDIENTS

4 oz whole-wheat bread crumbs
2 handfuls of parsley, chopped
handful of chives, chopped
4–6 tablespoons butter
3 oz mushrooms, finely chopped
3 thin slices of unsmoked bacon, finely
*   chopped*
2 eggs
salt and pepper
6 veal escalopes or cutlets
6 thin slices of unsmoked bacon, halved

Mix the bread crumbs with the parsley and chives in a bowl. Melt 2 tablespoons of the butter and fry the mushrooms and chopped bacon gently for 3 to 4 minutes, then add them to the bread crumbs with the eggs and seasoning. Mix together well.

Butter the middle of six sheets of parchment paper with the remaining butter and lay a cutlet or escalope lengthwise on it. Divide the stuffing into six portions and lay one on the top of each piece of meat. Then cover the stuffing with the halved bacon slices. Fold up the packages – you should be able to fold the paper over lengthwise a couple of times, then twist the ends around as though you were making a cracker. If that does not work, just fold the ends under as for an ordinary package. Lay the packages in a well oiled baking sheet or large frying pan, cover and cook gently for 45 to 60 minutes depending on the thickness of the meat. If cooking the packages in the oven, the temperature should be around 325°.

When ready, put each package on a dish and open up the middle a little if possible so you can see what is inside. Garnish with a sprig of watercress or whatever else is available at the time (I used sage flowers) and serve with two or three cooked vegetables (I served green beans, new potatoes and baby leeks). The *papillotes* should not need any extra sauce.

VEGETABLES

Although the Aristologist is warm in his praise of vegetables he gives few recipes for actually cooking them. He notes that "all kinds of vegetables are excellent stewed," and that "a small bit of charcoal or a little sugar boiled with any vegetable will counteract its bitter taste." He also goes into some detail about when you should boil (new) and when you should steam potatoes. Of purées he says:
"This is generally the French preparation of vegetables, and the mode is merely to pulp the vegetables through a sieve and add a little stock or water."

Apart from that he praises a Raised Vegetable Pie as being superior to a meat one (see opposite) – and passes on to salads:

"SALADS   There is nothing more wholesome than vegetable salads, and there is no question that they promote digestion, when eaten with moderation. Lettuce, endive, cold potatoes, mild raw onions, and beet, when properly dressed, with good vinegar and the best salad oil, not forgetting pepper, both red and black, are excellent in their way. We have read that some years since an Italian *artiste* made professional visits to the houses of the nobility and gentry of London for the purpose of dressing their salads. He rode in his carriage, after the manner of fashionable physicians, and his *fee* was one guinea. The materials he provided himself, and would allow no one to witness his compounding. His preparations were not always the same, but suited to the palate of his employers; and during the season he realised from forty to fifty guineas per day. Subsequently the 1s. 6d. mixture compounded by Batty, which would make a dozen salads, spoiled the foreigner's trade, and he was obliged to 'shut up.'"

RAISED VEGETABLE PIE

Serves 6 to 8

"Any kind of meat, poultry or game," says Abbott, "may be put into raised pies. Sometimes the crust is made hard and ornamental in a mould called a timbale; on other occasions the crust is made for eating. Raised pies of vegetables alone are an exquisite dish." I made a pie following Abbott's own recipe for raised pie paste and came to the conclusion that it must have been intended as ornamental rather than edible! Instead I suggest you use the recipe for "Mrs. —'s Pastry – the receipt of an elegant Australian lady, whose fair hands could fabricate by this simple mode, crust infinitely superior to any professional daubing; and as a matter of course, its intrinsic goodness was wonderfully enhanced if the eater was acquainted with the maker."

I have given the alternative of reduced quantities for the pastry in case you prefer to use a deep pie dish and just top the pie with the paste.

INGREDIENTS

6 cups (or 2 cups for topped pie) whole-
*   wheat flour*
⅔ cup (or ¼ cup for topped pie) butter
2 eggs (or 1 small for topped pie),
*   beaten*
about ⅔ cup (or 2–4 tablespoons for
*   topped pie) warm water*

FILLING

1½ lb assorted "unjuicy" vegetables
1 cup roughly chopped tomatoes
sea salt and freshly ground black
*   pepper*

Note You can use onions, carrots, turnips, parsnips, beets, cauliflower, broccoli, mushrooms, baby corn, chicory, sprouts, celery, potatoes, beans (fava, green, etc.) – or any others that take your fancy.

Make the pastry by rubbing the fats into the flour until it becomes sandy. Add the eggs and enough water to make a firm dough.

Cut the vegetables into roughly similarly sized pieces and steam them until *just* beginning to soften – you will obviously have to start some before the others but you should be able to cook them all in the same steamer, putting the softer vegetables on top of the harder ones. When the vegetables are cooked, turn them into a bowl, mix them with the tomatoes and season them very thoroughly with sea salt and freshly ground black pepper.

For the raised pie, roll out two thirds of the dough and line a 6–7 inch cake pan with a removable base or a raised pie mold with removable sides. Turn the vegetables into the lined pie mold if you are making a raised pie, or into a pie dish just big enough to hold them if it is only to be topped. Roll out the remaining dough in either case and cover the pie. Garnish it with pastry leaves or balls and brush it with a little egg, if you wish.

Bake the topped pie at 375° for 20 to 25 minutes, or until the pastry is crisp and lightly browned. The raised pie should be baked for rather longer (35 to 40 minutes) at a slightly lower temperature to allow the walls to cook without burning the top. Serve the pies either hot or cold.

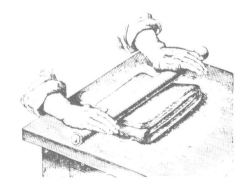

"CHAPTER XXV – THE DESSERT"

"'A word of doubtful etymology, signifying the last service at dinner, consisting of fruits and confections and etc. The modern dessert is probably equivalent to the *mensae secundae* of the Romans. In all countries of Europe the splendour of the dessert has ever since the period of its introduction kept pace with the progress of refinement and civilisation; and by many gastronomes the qualities and arrangement of a dessert are looked upon as the most valid test of all that is Attic in taste, and refined in elegance.' Brande.

"There is no question," Abbott continues, "that Professor Brande is correct in the above definition of a dessert, as nothing adds so much to a banquet, or the most ordinary dinner party, than that the last course should be perfect of it kind. The amphitryon must see that this course is properly served and assorted. The arrangement is a mere matter of taste, perhaps display; but we have only now to enumerate the essentials, viz. cakes, biscuits, and conserves of every possible variety; ices, and fruits of every kind – pine apples, grapes, melons, strawberries, raspberries, cherries, plums, peaches, apricots, pears, apples, medlars, filberts, walnuts, chestnuts, oranges, shaddocks, figs, dates and many tropical varieties, not forgetting -

The simple olives, best allies of wine,
Must I pass over in my bill of fare?
I must, although a favourite *plat* of mine
In Spain, and Lucca, Athens, everywhere,
On them, and bread, 'twas oft my lot to dine.

"A LUXURY Frozen watermelon is all the rage among the epicures at Washington. The melon, subjected to the freezing process, should be buried in pounded ice, perhaps twelve hours previous to use, and packed away carefully in the coolest place attainable. When again brought to light the melon shows an even coating like dew upon its surface, and on being cut (lengthwise by all means) a smart, crisp detonation precedes the knife in its process when the fruit is in perfect condition. Then carve and eat *ad libitum*.' *Washington Evening Star*."

SUEDOISE OF PEACHES
Serves 6

This recipe is to be found in the chapter on Confectionery (that comes immediately after chapters on Cider and Perry and Ginger and before a twelve-line chapter on Fondus [*sic*] which is sort of logical for the Suedoise, but a bizarre place to find the Gooseberry Fool, Syllabub and Swiss Cream which accompany it. For once, Abbott has nothing to say about either peaches or the recipe – although it would have merited a little praise.

INGREDIENTS

6 large, ripe peaches plus 1½ lb other
  peaches (these do not need to be in
  such good condition)
1¼ cups water
¼ cup extra-fine sugar
juice of 1 lemon

Peel and halve or quarter the large peaches carefully. Put the water into a pan with the sugar, bring it to a boil slowly to allow the sugar to melt and cook it for 2 minutes. Lower in the peaches and simmer them for no more than 5 minutes. Lift them out with a perforated spoon, put them in a deep dish and pour half the syrup over them.

Peel and chop the remaining peaches and add them to the remaining syrup with the lemon juice. Bring the peaches back to a boil and simmer them gently for 45 minutes, making sure that they do not burn, until you have reduced them to a "marmalade." Lift the large peaches out of the syrup and reduce this by one half by boiling briskly for about 10 minutes – take care that it does not start to caramelize. Spoon the "marmalade" into a serving dish, arrange the halved or quartered peaches on it and pour over the reduced syrup. Abbott decorated his peaches with macaroons and pieces of candied citron or lemon peel, but I feel that maybe they are better left virgin. Serve with or without cream as you fancy.

SUEDOISE OF PEACHES

RICE CAKES
Makes 15 to 20 cakes

Given Abbott's opinion that "breakfast should be the principal meal of the day" it is not surprising that he devotes several pages to "Bread and Breakfast cakes" – these include the infamous "damper." Among them is this excellent recipe for rice cakes (a rice version of a potato cake) that can be made in advance and reheated and that are, as he says, "easily digestible."

INGREDIENTS

⅔ cup white rice
4 tablespoons butter
1¼ cups milk
3 eggs
scant 1¼ cups whole-wheat flour

Cook the rice in boiling water until it is absolutely soft; drain it and mix in the butter. Allow the rice and butter to cool completely, then stir in the milk. Beat the eggs with the flour and beat into the rice mixture gradually, keeping it as smooth as possible. Heat a little oil on a griddle or in a large flat pan and drop tablespoons of the mixture on to cook briskly. When well tanned on one side, turn and cook on the other side. Serve hot with lots of butter.

STOCKS AND SAUCES

Stocks and sauces were immensely important to the Victorian cook as they formed the base of almost every savory dish he or she prepared. Any cook with any pretensions toward expertise always expected therefore to have a supply of the basic stocks and sauces ready for use in the larder. Moreover, it was widely recognized that the quality of the finished dish depended on the quality of the stock. As Francatelli says on the first page of *The Modern Cook:*
"Although great care and watchful attention are requisite in every branch of the culinary art, the exercise of these qualities is most essential in the preparation of the grand stock sauces [brown stock or consommé and white stock]. If the first process which these undergo be not successfully effected, no subsequent care will remedy the mischief."

COMMON OR GRAND STOCK FOR GENERAL PURPOSES

(FRANCATELLI)
Makes about 3¾ quarts

INGREDIENTS

a knuckle of veal, well broken up
2 beef marrow bones, if obtainable,
broken up
3¾ quarts water
1 lb chuck beef
2 carrots, chopped
2 turnips, chopped
2 celery stalks, chopped
2 leeks, chopped
salt

Put the veal and bones into a large pan, pour on the water and bring to the boil, gradually, removing any scum which may rise to the surface. When all the scum has risen, add the vegetables and a little salt, bring it all back to a boil and simmer gently for 7 hours. Alternatively, it could be cooked in a slow cookpot for 12 hours. When it is cooked, pass the liquid through a fine strainer and store it for future use.

GOOD WHITE STOCK

(MRS. BEETON)
Makes about 2½ quarts

INGREDIENTS

about 2 lb knuckle of veal
a few chicken bones
2 slices of lean ham
1 tablespoon butter
2½ quarts water
1 carrot, roughly chopped
1 medium onion, roughly chopped
3 celery stalks, chopped
6 white peppercorns or ¼ teaspoon
ground white pepper
1 teaspoon salt
1 blade mace or ¼ teaspoon ground
mace

Put the veal, chicken bones, ham and butter in a large pan with 1¼ cups of the water and cook briskly until "the gravy flows." Then add the remaining ingredients, bring to a boil slowly and simmer very gently, covered, for 5 hours. If you are using a slow cookpot, transfer the veal mixture to it before adding the remaining ingredients and make sure the water is boiling. It could then be cooked overnight. Strain the stock and allow to cool, then chill in the refrigerator and remove the fat from the top before using.

ESPAGNOLE (BROWN SAUCE)

(ELIZA ACTON)
Makes about 2½ cups

Francatelli gives immensely complicated recipes for both velouté and Espagnole. To my mind, Eliza Acton, who reduces both to manageable proportions, is a better bet.

INGREDIENTS

2 tablespoons butter
2 shallots, preferably, or 1 small onion,
    roughly chopped
1 carrot, roughly chopped
¾ cup roughly chopped lean ham
2 parsley stalks, bay leaves and
    branches of thyme or 2 bouquets
    garnis
3 cloves
blade of mace
12 peppercorns
2½ cups white stock

Melt the butter in a pan and fry the vegetables, ham and herbs gently until they are well colored all over but not burned. Add the stock gradually, scraping any bits carefully from the bottom of the pan as you add the liquid. Bring to a boil and simmer gently for 40 minutes. Strain the sauce, skim off any excess fat and set aside.

VELOUTE

(ELIZA ACTON)
Makes about 3¾ cups

INGREDIENTS

2½ cups white stock
2½ cups heavy cream
salt and ground white pepper

Put the stock and cream in separate pans. Bring the stock to a boil and boil briskly for 20 to 30 minutes to reduce it by at least one third. Bring the cream to a boil and simmer it for 10 minutes to reduce by about one quarter. Mix the two together and adjust seasoning to taste with salt and ground white pepper. Set aside for further use.

BECHAMEL SAUCE

(FRANCATELLI)
Makes about 2½ cups

INGREDIENTS

2 tablespoons butter
¼ cup all-purpose flour
1½ cups good chicken or veal stock
¾ cup heavy cream
1 carrot, sliced
2 bouquets garnis
salt and white pepper
pinch of nutmeg

Melt the butter in a pan, add the flour and cook for 2 minutes without coloring. Add the stock and cream gradually, stirring continuously, and cook until the sauce has thickened slightly. Add the carrot, bouquets garnis and seasoning and simmer for 20 minutes, stirring frequently to make sure the sauce does not burn. If the sauce is not totally smooth, pass it through a fine strainer and reserve for use.

BEEF GRAVY

(MRS. BEETON)
Makes about 5 cups

INGREDIENTS

½ lb lean beef
5 cups water
1 onion, roughly chopped
salt and pepper
1 teaspoon arrowroot
2 tablespoons mushroom catsup

Cut up the beef in medium-size chunks. Put into a pan or slow cooker with the water and onion and season generously. Bring it to a boil and simmer very gently for 3 hours. Alternatively, it could be cooked overnight in a slow cookpot. Strain the gravy and discard the beef and onions. Mix the arrowroot with the mushroom catsup, stir into the gravy and continue to cook for a few minutes until it thickens slightly. Adjust the seasoning to taste before using.

A DINNER IN IMPERIAL INDIA

W e are only now beginning to realize how very difficult life must have been for the English memsahibs who "went out" to India during the long years of Victoria's reign. They certainly had plenty of servants and little to do, but they also had to contend with appalling heat, particularly in the south, total lack of modern amenities, insanitary conditions, little medical help, and often almost total isolation. Add to this a pack of Indian servants whose roles and language they did not understand, and food and a tradition of cookery which were utterly foreign, and often distasteful to them, and one can understand how welcome Colonel Kenney Herbert's *Culinary Jottings* must have been and why these went into five editions in almost as many years.

The Colonel, who wrote under the pen name of Wyvern, spent thirty-two years in India, before returning to England at the turn of the century to start a Commonsense Cookery Association and school, and write for various magazines on the subjects of dining, cooking and household management. Like other army cooks, the Colonel is a model of precision, accuracy and common sense. Not only are his recipes precise and easy to follow but his advice is always reliable; he has a truly military lack of patience with "fol-de-rols" and fripperies, and no time at all for what he regards as the failings of cooks or their mistresses in whatever department of household management he is dealing with. His article on Indian kitchens, for example, originally published in the *Madras Mail*, thunders down the years with all the righteousness of deep offense:

"Remembering as we all can so well the cheerful

aspect of the English kitchen, its trimness, its comfort and its cleanliness, how comes it to pass that in India we continue year after year to be fully aware that the chamber set apart for the preparation of our food is, in ninety nine cases out of a hundred, the foulest in our premises – and are not ashamed? . . . Over and over again have revolting facts been discovered in connection with the habits and customs of the cook room. But instead of striking at the root of the evil, and taking vigorous action to inaugurate reform, we are absolutely callous enough not only to tolerate barbarisms, but even to speak of the most abominable practices as jests!"

By the time the Colonel was making his culinary jottings, the Indian empire had started to change. Improved transport enabled a greatly increased quantity of European goods to find their way to Bombay, Delhi or Madras, while the ever larger English communities, particularly in the cities, allowed for the growth of a proper "social round." With this growing Europeanization the old Indian habits of eating curry and mulligatunny had been pushed out of fashion. As the Colonel says in his introduction:

"Our dinner today would indeed astonish our Anglo Indian forefathers. With a taste for light wines and a far more moderate indulgence in stimulating drinks, has been germinated a desire for delicate and artistic cookery. Quality has superseded quantity, and the molten curries and florid oriental compositions of the olden time – so fearfully and wonderfully made – have been gradually banished from our dinner tables."

Given that the "florid compositions" were the only thing that "Ramasamy" really knew how to prepare, it is not surprising that "the want of a handbook on culinary science of a modern description . . . must long have been felt by the busy housewives of Madras."

The result is that in all the Colonel's five

OPPOSITE: MULLIGATUNNY SOUP AND RAISED GAME PIE

hundred odd pages, only about forty-five are devoted to what we would think of as Indian cooking. The rest deal with European dishes, overwhelmingly French in inspiration, but using a judicious selection from and adaptation of local ingredients. Indeed, some of the Colonel's tartest comments are reserved for those ladies who insist on serving expensive and unappetizing canned English vegetables instead of the excellent fresh vegetables obtainable year round.

The book is divided into two sections, the first being devoted to his comments on cooking in general, with a few recipes thrown in mainly as illustration. The second section contains thirty menus for parties of eight, six and "little home dinners," each with the appropriate recipes. Although he says he will "treat of cosy, sociable little dinners of from two to ten people, rather than of the elaborate banquets of the great," most of the menus would defeat the modern cook. But fascinating and excellent though the recipes are, the more interesting part of the book is the general advice on all branches of cooking. Much of its charm must lie both in the humor of the author and in the insight it gives into the society for which he wrote – in particular its dealings with "Ramasamy," the native cook:

"I place those who have not patience the first on the list of persons whom I deem incapable of managing their cooks. I do so advisedly, for of all failings inimical to the successful direction of native servants, a hasty temper is the most fatal. The moment you betray irritation and hastiness in your manner towards Ramasamy, he ceases to follow you. His brain becomes busy in the consultation of his personal safety, and not in the consideration of the *plat* you may be endeavouring to discuss with him ... All native cooks dearly love the spice box, and they all reverence 'Worcester sauce.' Now I consider the latter too powerful an element by far for indiscriminate use. If in the house at all, the proper place for this sauce is in the cruet stand where it can be seized in an emergency to drown mistakes. But it should be preserved from Ramasamy with the same studious care as a bottle of chloroform from a lady suffering from acute neuralgia."

However, the advice the Colonel gives is interesting and pertinent even to the modern cook. To illustrate the precision of his style I shall quote in full his description of the omelet made for him by a "Member of the Madras Civil Ser-

vice at a place called Pennaconda, as I was marching with a Regiment from Bangalore to Secunderabad:

"Calling for a slop basin he broke into it four ordinary country fowl's eggs whole, and added the yolks of only two more. These he thoroughly *mixed* by using two forks; he did not *beat them at all*. When thoroughly satisfied that the incorporation had been effected, he flavoured the mixture with a salt spoonful of salt, a teaspoonful of very finely minced shallot, a heaped up tablespoonful of minced curly parsley (grown in his garden) and – to crown all a tablespoonful of really rich cream. He stirred this a minute ... We now left the dining room for the verandah where there was a good charcoal fire in an iron brasier, and upon it a pan about ten inches in diameter, very shalllow, with a narrow rim well sloped outwards. A pat of butter was melted in the pan, sufficient in quantity to thoroughly lubricate the whole of its surface, and leave a coating of moisture about an eighth of an inch deep over all. As soon as it was ready, quite burning hot, – the butter having ceased to splutter and beginning to brown, – with one good stir round, the mixture was poured into the pan. At the moment of contact, the underpart of the *omelette* formed, this was instantly lifted by the spoon, and the unformed portion allowed to run beneath it; the left hand holding the pan, and playing it, as it were, from side to side: With one good shake the pan (*in less than one minute from the commencing of operation*) was lifted from the fire, and its contents rolled off into the hot silver dish at hand to receive it. The *omelette,* as it rolled of its own accord from the pan, caught up, and buried within it, the slightly unformed juicy part of the mixture which still remained on the surface; and as it lay in the dish, was without an special shape, of a golden yellow colour, flecked with green, with the juicy part escaping from beneath its folds."

Following the success of *Culinary Jottings,* (1878), the first of his cookbooks, Colonel Kenney Herbert continued to write until and after his retirement to England. Of his personal life, as one might expect of such a classically military character, we know virtually nothing, but his personality speaks loud and clear from every one of the five hundred and thirteen pages of his "Treatise on Reformed Cookery for Anglo Indian Exiles."

MULLIGATUNNY

Serves 8

"... This preparation, originally peculiar to Southern India, derives its name from two Tamil words – *molegoo* (pepper) and *tunnee* (water). In its simple form, as partaken of by the poorer natives of Madras, it is, as its name indicates, a 'pepper water' or *soupe maigre,* which Mootoosamy makes as follows:

He pounds together a tablespoon of tamarind, six red chillies, six cloves of garlic, a teaspoonful of mustard seed, a salt spoonful of fenugreek seed, twelve black peppercorns, a teaspoonful of salt and six leaves of *karay-pauk.* When worked to a paste he adds a pint of water, and boils the mixture for a quarter of an hour. While this is going on he cuts up two small onions, puts them into a chatty, and fries them in a dessertspoonful of ghee till they begin to turn brown, when he strains the pepper water into the chatty, and cooks the mixture for five minutes after which it is ready. The pepper water is eaten with a large quantity of boiled rice and it's a meal in itself.

"The English, taking their ideas from this simple composition, added other condiments, with chicken, mutton and etc and thickened the liquid with flour and butter, and by degrees, succeeded in concocting a *soupe grasse* of a decidedly acceptable kind. Oddly enough we undoubtedly get the best *mulligatunny* nowadays in England where it is presented in the form of a clear as well as that of a thick, soup. From an artistic point of view, the former is infinitely the better of the two . . ."

INGREDIENTS

½ lb lean ham
2 lb leg or neck of veal, with bones
2 lb lean stew beef
2 tablespoons butter
2 quarts boiling water
2½ cups cold water
2 teaspoons salt
1 onion, chopped
1 carrot, chopped
1 turnip, chopped
3 celery stalks, chopped
2 bouquets garnis
6 cloves
6 white peppercorns
2 large blades of mace
½ cup coriander seed
¼ cup cumin seed
¼ cup fenugreek
3 tablespoons mustard seed
2 garlic cloves, chopped
2 black peppercorns
5 cilantro leaves
Tabasco

Cut the various meats into thick slices. Melt the butter in a large pan and fry the meats until they are all well browned, taking care that they do not burn. Add the bones and pour in the boiling water gradually. Bring back to a boil and skim carefully as the scum rises. Add the cold water gradually to help the scum to rise. When all the scum has been removed, add the vegetables, bouquets garnis, cloves, peppercorns and mace, and let the soup boil gently for 5½ to 6 hours. Alternatively, you could cook it in a slow cookpot overnight.

Pass the liquid carefully through a fine strainer, lined, if possible, with cheesecloth. Allow the consommé to get completely cold, then remove every bit of fat from the top. Transfer the consommé to a clean pan with a ladle, taking care not to disturb any of the sediment at the bottom.

Tie the remaining spices in a cheesecloth bag or infuser and lower them into the consommé. Bring to a boil and simmer very gently for 30 minutes. Leave to cool completely. Discard the spices and reheat the mulligatunny to serve. Add a dash of Tabasco to each portion as served.

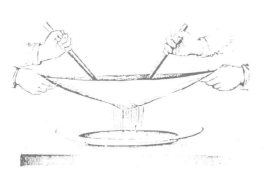

BROILED FISH EN PAPILLOTES

Serves 8

"'Fish, under skilful hands, offers,' says Brillat Savarin, 'inexhaustible resources of gustatory enjoyment.' And we, who live at Madras, on a coast which yields a perennial supply of good fish, should surely lay these words to heart . . . But do we avail ourselves of the many opportunities we possess of turning Madras fish to good account? I certainly think not. At the ordinary Madras dinner party you may only rely on having boiled seer fish, with a sauce and a few slices of cucumber and beetroot, or a spoonful of salad, on the side of your plate. I have never been able to trace the origin of this Madras custom of serving a portion of *salad* with a thick eggy dressing on the same plate as a slice of *hot* fish. To put salad on a *hot* plate to begin with is an unpardonable offence, while the association of salad with *hot fish* is incongruous in the extreme.

"Broiling fish sounds simple, but under this head there are a few toothsome recipes not to be despised."

INGREDIENTS

8 fillets of white fish or salmon
½ cup olive, nut or good vegetable oil
5 shallots or scallions, minced
2 large garlic cloves, crushed
large handful of parsley, chopped
¼ cup wine vinegar
grated peel of 2 limes or substitute 1
  large lemon
salt and pepper

Note The Colonel used seer fish that he describes as "a large salmon-shaped fish, which is cut up and sold in much the same manner as salmon and is susceptible of being similarly cooked," but cod or haddock will do excellently.

Put the fish in a flattish pan or microwave dish, cover it with boiling water and simmer for 5 minutes on the stove or 2 minutes in a microwave. Remove and drain carefully. Mix all the other ingredients thoroughly in a large enough glass or porcelain dish to hold the fish comfortably. Lay the fish on top of the marinade, then spoon over the excess to make sure the fillets are well immersed. Cover and leave for 6 to 12 hours.

To cook his fish, the Colonel wrapped it, with its marinade, in "well oiled papers and broiled it over a fast, clear fire." I found it easier to lay the fish with the marinade in an ample bed of foil and to cover them with well-oiled wax paper. The fish can then be cooked under a hot broiler, in a wide heavy frying pan or on a barbecue, for between 6 and 8 minutes, depending on the thickness of the fillets.

The Colonel suggests that the fish are served in their marinade with "a nice sharp brown sauce like *sauce Robert*," but I found that the sauce killed the flavor of the fish and the marinade. If you do want to follow the Colonel's advice, use the Espagnole sauce on page 145 as a base. Then sharpen it to taste with 2 tablespoons each of wine vinegar and French mustard and a pinch each of sugar and salt.

OPPOSITE: BROILED SALMON EN PAPILLOTE

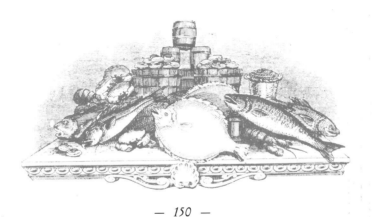

CURRY

"We are often told by men of old time, whose long connection with the country entitles them to speak with the confidence of 'fellows who know, don't you know,' that in inverse proportion, as it were, to the steady advance of civilisation in India, the sublime art of curry making has gradually passed from the Indian cook ... Looking back myself to the hour of my arrival in India, I call to mind the kind hearted veteran who threw his doors open to me. It rejoiced him, I remember, to give 'tiffin' parties at which he prided himself on sending round eight or nine varieties of curries, with divers platters of freshly made chutneys, grilled ham, preserved roes of fishes, etc. The discussion of the 'course' – a little banquet in itself – used to occupy at least half an hour for it was the correct thing to taste each curry, and to call for those that specially gratified you a second time. Now this, my friend, was, I take it, a type of the last Anglo Indian generation; a generation that fostered the art of curry making, and bestowed as much attention to it as we, in these days of grace [1878], do to copying the culinary triumphs of the lively Gaul ...

"Curries nowadays are only licensed to be eaten at breakfast, at luncheon and perhaps at the little home dinner, when they may, for a change, occasionally form the *pièce de résistance* of that cosy meal."

The Colonel went on to bemoan the fact that since curries had fallen from favor, few people were prepared to take the time to prepare their powders and pastes properly, turning instead to inferior "store-bought" brands ... He then gives his own basic curry powder and paste recipes (right) and a selection of curries that can be made from them. He suggests making a large batch, but I have reduced the quantities to more manageable proportions.

When making his curry powder the Colonel seldom had the benefit of ready ground spices and therefore had to dry, parch, clean and sieve them all before they were pounded and sifted. As he points out, many whole seeds (coriander and cumin, for example) lose much weight in the sifting process. Although the flavor would be marginally better if it were possible to use all whole seeds and roots in the preparation of the powder, in the interests of simplicity and convenience I am suggesting that you use ready-ground spices.

"STOCK" CURRY POWDER
Makes about 3 cups

INGREDIENTS

½ cup ground turmeric
½ cup ground coriander
⅓ cup ground cumin
¼ cup poppy seeds
½ cup fenugreek
¼ cup ground ginger
3 tablespoons mustard seed
¼ cup dried red chilis
⅓ cup ground black pepper
1 heaped teaspoon salt

Put all the ingredients into a food processor and grind finely. Store in airtight jars.

"STOCK" CURRY PASTE
Makes about 1½ cups

INGREDIENTS

2 small onions, chopped
2 garlic cloves, chopped
1 tablespoon ground turmeric
4 teaspoons coriander seed
4 teaspoons poppy seed
1 tablespoon sugar
1 tablespoon salt
2 teaspoons ground black pepper
2 heaped teaspoons grated fresh ginger
*   root*
generous pinch of ground cinnamon
¾ cup grated fresh, or shredded,
*   coconut*
¾ cup ground almonds
juice of 2 limes or substitute 1 large
*   lemon*

Put all the ingredients into a food processor and grind finely, then store in an airtight jar.

CHICKEN CURRY

Serves 8

INGREDIENTS

*1 large chicken or capon, jointed and
  dredged with flour*
*¾ cup ground almonds or 1¾ cups
  shredded coconut*
2½ cups boiling water
1 stick plus 1 tablespoon butter
3 large onions, sliced
3 large garlic cloves, finely chopped
*3 tablespoons "stock" curry powder
  (see left)*
*3 tablespoons "stock" curry paste (see
  left)*
3 shallots or 5 scallions, finely chopped
5 bay leaves
5 sprigs of fresh cilantro
3 tablespoons red currant jelly
juice of 3 limes or substitute 2 lemons
1 heaped tablespoon good chutney

Note The Colonel suggests that a pinch of
ground cloves, mace, cinnamon, nutmeg, carda-
mom or allspice may be added to the curry mixture if liked. However, "a salt spoon of one, or at
the most two, of these aromatic powders
blended, will suffice for a large curry. Dr. Kitchiner's precept viz: that the mixing of several
spices is a blunder, should never be forgotten."
He also suggests "green leaves that are often useful when judiciously introduced are: fennel,
lemon grass, bay leaves and green coriander
[cilantro]."

Use the bones and trimmings of the chicken, with
2½ cups water, to make chicken stock.

Meanwhile, pour the boiling water over the
almonds or coconut and leave to stand for 10
minutes, then strain. Melt the stick of butter in a
large, wide pan, big enough to hold the chicken,
and fry the onion and garlic until they turn
yellow. Add the curry powder and paste and
cook for a few more minutes, stirring continuously. Add 2 cups of the almond or coconut milk
and the stock gradually and simmer the mixture
for 15 minutes.

Melt the remaining butter in another pan and
fry the shallot or scallions for a few minutes, then
add the chicken and fry gently until lightly
browned all over. Transfer the chicken to the

curry mixture, coat thoroughly and marinate for
30 minutes. Add the bay and cilantro leaves, red
currant jelly, lime or lemon juice and chutney
and simmer very gently for 30 minutes. Finally,
remove the bay and cilantro leaves and add the
remaining coconut or almond milk just before
the curry is served with lots of boiled Basmati or
Patna rice.

ROGNONS EN SURPRISE

Serves 8

This dish appears in one of the Colonel's
"Menus" – "a most excellent savoury entremet,
if carefully done." I have served it very successfully with Riz à la Ménagère (page 154).

INGREDIENTS

8 fairly large onions
about 4 tablespoons butter
*4 lamb's kidneys, trimmed and fairly
  finely diced*
4 large anchovies, very finely chopped
large handful of parsley, finely chopped
salt and pepper
1 lime or small lemon
about 2½ cups brown sauce (page 145)

Peel the onions, leaving as much of their tops and
tails on as possible, then boil them for about 25
minutes in plenty of well salted water – they
should be about three quarters cooked. Trim the
roots so that they stand upright and cut enough
from the tops to allow you to gouge out the
middle of each onion. Purée the insides of the
onions with 2 tablespoons of the butter.

Mix the kidneys with the anchovies and
parsley and season lightly. Put a little of the
onion purée into the bottom of each onion.
Divide the kidney mixture in eight portions and
pack one into each onion. Add a small knob of
butter and a squeeze of lime or lemon juice to
each onion, then cover with the remaining onion
purée. Put the onions in a buttered ovenproof
dish and cover with foil or a lid. Bake at 350° for 1
hour. To serve, remove the onions to a serving
dish and pour over some of the brown sauce;
serve the rest of the sauce separately.

RICE

"... there are very few establishments in India in which a day passes without the preparation of rice for the table. It is, as a rule, served plainly boiled ... For those who may like to know how the task is performed, here is the recipe:
Having thoroughly sifted and cleansed the rice, cast it into *boiling* water with a pinch of sugar, a salt spoonful of salt and the juice of a quarter of a lime. Stir the grains as they are cooking with a wooden spoon every now and then, and in about twelve minutes test them by taking of a few grains out of the water, and pinching them between finger and thumb. As soon as the grain is tender, check the boiling by a dash of cold water, remove the vessel from the fire, and invert it, holding the rice securely with the lid yet leaving space for the escape of the water. When quite dry, re-invert the pan, shaking the well drained grains of rice in the hot vessel ... Lastly cover the pan with a clean cloth, and let it rest on the hot plate to complete the drying."

RIZ A LA MENAGERE
Serves 8

INGREDIENTS

1 cup Basmati or Patna rice
⅔ cup diced bacon
3 cups chicken or veal stock
pinch of pepper
2 tablespoons tomato paste
¼ cup white wine
¾ cup water
chopped parsley to garnish

Rinse the rice and cook it in plenty of boiling water for 5 minutes; drain it.

Meanwhile, fry the bacon dice in a wide stewing pan, in their own fat, until they start to turn yellow. Add the rice with the stock and the pepper and simmer for 15 minutes, stirring occasionally, or until the rice is cooked. Mix the tomato paste with the wine and water and add to the rice. Stir well and continue to cook until the sauce is heated through. Serve immediately sprinkled with the parsley.

FILET DE BOEUF A L'ITALIENNE
Serves 8

"Luncheon is a meal so popular among Britons both at Home and abroad, that the humblest treatise on cooking would be incomplete without a chapter specially dedicated to it. There are luncheons large and luncheons small. The former elaborate, very pleasant and sociable, yet alas! a little too alluring, and fatal in their effects upon the appetite for the rest of the day. The latter more enjoyable perhaps than their more ostentatious connections, for they are reserved for a few intimate friends, but affording just as much temptation to kill dinner.

"Here is a pretty little recipe for a *filet de boeuf à l'Italienne* which, to my mind, is worthy of attention, and well adapted to a midday festival."

If this classes as a "pretty little recipe" the mind boggles as to what the Colonel would class as a "major dish." Although he suggests using a fillet of beef ("the undercut of the sirloin if possible") I found that it was rather wasted on a dish that is to undergo long slow cooking. A good top round will serve the purpose a lot less expensively.

INGREDIENTS

⅔ cup very finely chopped mushrooms
2 handfuls of fresh parsley, finely chopped
½ medium onion, minced
freshly ground black pepper
2 thickish slices of lean, unsmoked back bacon
top round of beef, weighing about 6 lb
2 tablespoons butter
½ teaspoon dried thyme
½ teaspoon dried marjoram
grated rind of 1 lime or substitute 1 small lemon
1 garlic clove, crushed
1 medium onion, finely chopped
1 medium carrot, finely diced
2 tablespoons tomato paste
2⅓ cups beef or veal stock or consommé
1½ cups macaroni
1 tablespoon finely grated Cheddar cheese

SPINACH WITH SHORTBREAD (LEFT), CHICKEN CURRY (TOP),
FILET DE BOEUF A L'ITALIENNE AND RIZ A LA MENAGERE

Mix the mushrooms, parsley, onion and pepper and coat the slices of bacon. Cut an incision the length of the beef, lay in the coated bacon and tie the meat back into shape. Melt the butter in a heavy pan large enough to hold the beef and cook the herbs, rind, garlic, onion and carrot gently for 10 minutes. Place the meat on top of the vegetables. Mix the tomato paste with the stock or consommé and pour around the meat. Cover and cook very gently for 3 hours.

When you are ready to serve the meat, cook the macaroni in plenty of fast boiling water for about 10 minutes, or until it is cooked but still *al dente*. Drain it thoroughly and return it to the pan. Remove the meat on to a warmed serving dish and remove its ties; surround it with a few of the vegetables you intend to serve and pour over some of the cooking juices. Adjust the seasoning of the remaining juices to taste and add them, along with the vegetables and the grated cheese, to the macaroni. Mix all well together and turn on to a serving dish. Serve immediately. I served the beef with spinach (page 157) and small, lightly cooked carrots.

RAISED GAME PIE
Serves 8 to 10

"A good *Game Pie*," says the Colonel, "is a
capital thing for the luncheon or breakfast
party." You can use any combination of game
that you fancy as long as it is roughly equivalent
to the quantity given here. The recipe is rather
long and complicated – but worth it.

INGREDIENTS

1 pheasant
2 guinea fowl
2 wood pigeons
4 lamb chops, boned, well trimmed
    and cut in half
8 thin slices of bacon
¼ lb ham in one thick slice
6 large anchovy fillets

SPICED PEPPER

1 tablespoon thyme
1 tablespoon marjoram
1 tablespoon savory
2 tablespoons ground nutmeg
2 tablespoons ground cloves
pinch of ground black pepper
pinch of chilli or cayenne

STOCK

2 slices of fatty bacon
½ lb stewing beef (optional)
2 pigs' feet, if possible – especially if it
    is to be served cold
1 onion
1 carrot
1 celery stalk
mushroom stalks
2 bouquets garnis
1 garlic clove, chopped
12 peppercorns
⅔ cup Madeira or sweet sherry
1 tablespoon red wine vinegar
1 tablespoon red currant jelly
⅓ cup mushroom catsup

FORCEMEAT

livers of all the birds, or, if not
    available, ½ lb lambs' or chicken
    livers, diced
2 tablespoons ghee, clarified butter or
    good oil
2 slices of bacon, chopped
3 shallots or 4 scallions, chopped
¼ lb mushrooms, chopped
salt and pepper

PIE CRUST

2 cups whole-wheat flour
4½ oz butter or shortening
1 egg

Bone the birds and put the bones and all the trimmings into a largish pot. Make the spiced pepper by pounding all the ingredients together in a pestle and mortar or a small food processor. Coat the pieces of game liberally in the spiced pepper. Wrap each of the halved lamb chops in one piece of bacon. Cut the ham into largish fingers and chop the anchovies.

Put all the stock ingredients except the Madeira or sherry, vinegar, jelly and catsup into the large pan with the bones, just cover with water and bring to the boil. Simmer for 45 to 60 minutes, then strain and cool. Add the remaining ingredients. You will have far too much stock for the pie but the rest makes quite delicious soup, either hot or cold.

For the forcemeat, cook the diced livers with the bacon, shallots and mushrooms in the ghee or oil for 3 to 4 minutes, then purée in a food processor or blender, or rub through a strainer.

Make the pie crust by rubbing the fat into the flour, then adding water until you have a soft dough. Chill until needed.

Spread the forcemeat over the bottom and up the sides of a largish pie dish, just big enough to hold all the meat. Lay the lamb chops on the bottom, then fill the dish with the different pieces of game interspersed with the ham and the anchovies. If any spiced pepper remains, sprinkle it over the meat as you lay it in the dish.

When all the game is in the dish, roll out the pastry and cover the pie, leaving a couple of holes through which to add the stock. Keep the pastry trimmings.

Cook the pie at 300° for 1½ hours. Add sufficient stock through a funnel to come most of the way up the meat and then use the remaining pastry to cover the holes and garnish the pie. Glaze with the beaten egg and return to a slightly hotter oven at 350° for a further 20 minutes to finish cooking the pastry. The pie can be served hot or cold, although the latter is probably more manageable!

SPINACH WITH SHORTBREAD
Serves 8

"... With common care, no *entremets de légumes* are more delicate than those which we can achieve with this vegetable [spinach]."

INGREDIENTS

¼ cup melted butter
⅓ cup all-purpose flour
1 scant teaspoon salt
pinch of sugar
¼ cup sharp grated cheese
4 lb fresh spinach, well washed,
    thoroughly drained and with any
    heavy stalks removed
4 tablespoons butter
5 tablespoons all-purpose flour
pinch of salt
pinch of sugar
1¼ cups milk, chicken or veal stock or
    brown gravy

Mix the melted butter into the flour, add the salt, sugar and cheese and mix to a soft dough. Roll out on a well-floured board, cut into hearts or other shapes and bake at 350° for 10 minutes. Set aside.

Cook the spinach briefly in 2 inches boiling water, drain it thoroughly and chop it. Melt the butter in a large, wide pan, add the flour, salt and sugar and cook for a few minutes. Add the spinach and cook for a further 5 minutes. Then add the milk, stock or gravy and cook for a further 2 minutes to warm the sauce through. Turn on to a heated serving dish and garnish with the shortbread before serving.

PARFAIT OF CHOCOLATE
Serves 8

The average temperature in Madras was in the 90s, so the difficulties of making ice cream can only have been equaled by the pleasure of those lucky enough to be able to eat it. This pale and delicate parfait should be served just frozen, not icy solid.

INGREDIENTS

2 cups full cream milk or equal
    quantities milk and heavy cream
1 square semisweet chocolate, grated
⅓ cup extra-fine sugar
5 egg yolks
1 envelope gelatin, dissolved in 2
    tablespoons boiling water
3 drops of vanilla extract
1¼ cups heavy cream

Put the milk, chocolate and 2 tablespoons of the sugar into a pan and heat gradually until the chocolate melts. Meanwhile, beat the egg yolks, then beat in the chocolate milk gradually. Cook over a very gentle heat until the custard thickens slightly but take care not to let it curdle. Whisk the dissolved gelatin into the custard, then cool it. Make a syrup from the remaining sugar, the vanilla and 6 tablespoons boiling water, then leave to cool. When both are cold, mix the syrup into the custard.

If you have an ice cream machine, whip the cream lightly, mix it with the custard and syrup and freeze-churn in your machine. When the ice cream is frozen but still soft enough to handle, transfer it into an oiled fancy or ring mold and finish freezing in a freezer compartment. If you do not have a machine, put the custard and syrup mixture into the freezer and when it is starting to freeze, take it out and mix it with the lightly whipped cream. Pour into a mold and freeze as above. Although the ice cream should turn out properly if the mold has been oiled, you may prefer to play safe by lining the mold with plastic wrap. To serve turn the mold out on to a decorative plate 15 to 20 minutes before you want to eat it and serve with small cookies.

GATEAU DE PISTACHE
Serves 8

In the "notes" that precede his "menus," the Colonel says of desserts: "I have not attempted to treat of *sweet dishes* in this work, but the *entremets sucrés* chosen for each bill of fare have been carefully described."

INGREDIENTS

4 eggs
the weight of 3 of the eggs in
*   confectioners' sugar*
the weight of 1 of the eggs in potato
*   flour, or substitute all-purpose flour*
the weight of 1 of the eggs in shelled
*   pistachio nuts*
½ egg white
scant ½ cup confectioners' sugar
juice of about ½ lime or small lemon

Grind the pistachio nuts very finely in a food processor or with a pestle and mortar. Separate the eggs and beat the yolks with the sugar until they become white and creamy. Whisk the egg whites until they are stiff, then beat in half the egg yolks with half the flour. Beat in the remaining flour, then fold in the remaining egg white with the pistachio nuts. Spoon the mixture into a lined or loose-based 8 inch pan and bake at 300° for 35 minutes.

Meanwhile, mix the remaining sugar with enough egg white and lime juice to make a fairly stiff paste – like a thick batter. When the cake is cooked, remove it from the oven and spread the paste gently over the top. Return it to the oven for a further 7 to 10 minutes to set the paste. The cake can be further decorated with strips of citron peel and candied cherries as soon as it comes out of the oven. Cool slightly, then remove carefully from the pan and cool on a rack. Serve cold.

BIBLIOGRAPHY

Abbott, Edward. *The English and Australian Cook Book*, 1864.
Acton, Eliza. *Modern Cookery for Private Families*, Longmans Green, 1845, facsimile Elek Books, 1966.
    The English Bread Book, Longmans Green, 1852.
Barr, Pat. *The Memsahibs: The Women of Victorian India*, Secker & Warburg, 1976.
Beeton, Isabella. *The Book of Household Management*, 1861, facsimile Jonathan Cape, 1968.
Cooper-English, Colin and Bridge, Tom. *W.M. Kitchiner, MD, and the Cook's Oracle*, Lennard, 1989.
Davidson, Caroline. *A Woman's Work is Never Done*, Chatto & Windus, 1982.
Drummond, J.C. and Wilbraham, Anne. *The Englishman's Food*, Jonathan Cape, 1939, revised 1957.
Farmer, Fannie. *The Boston Cooking School Cookbook*, 1896, facsimile Plume, 1974.
    A Book of Good Dinners for my Friend, 1905.
    Food and Cookery for the Sick and Convalescent, 1907.
    Catering for Special Occasions, 1911.
    A New Book of Cookery, 1912.
Francatelli, Charles. *The Modern Cook*, 1846, facsimile Dover and Constable, 1973.
    A Plain Cookery Book for the Working Classes, 1852, facsimile Scolar Press.
    The Good Cook's Guide and Butler's Assistant, 1861.
    The Royal English and Foreign Confectionery Book, 1862.
Fussell, G.E. and K.R. *The English Countrywoman*, Melrose, 1953; Orbis, 1981.
    The English Countryman, Melrose, 1955; Orbis, 1981.
Harrison, Molly. *The Kitchen in History*, Osprey, 1972.
Hartley, Dorothy. *Food in England*, Macdonald, 1954.
Horn, Pamela. *The Victorian Servant*, Gill & Macmillan, 1975; Alan Sutton, 1986.
Kettner, Auguste (E.S. Dallas). *The Book of the Table*, 1877; Centaur Press, 1968.

Kitchiner, William, MD. *The Cook's Oracle*, G.B. Whittaker, 1817.
Langley, Andrew (ed). *The Selected Soyer*, Absolute Press, 1987.
Morris, Helen. *Portrait of a Chef*, Cambridge University Press, 1938; Oxford University Press, 1980.
Nown, Graham. *Mrs Beeton: 150 Years of Cookery and Household Management*, Ward Lock, 1986.
Quennell, Peter (ed). *Mayhew's London: Selections from London Labour and the London Poor*, Pilot Press, 1949; William Kimber, 1950.
Ranhofer, Charles. *The Epicurean*, R. Ranhofer, 1893; facsimile Dover Publications, 1971.
Shapiro, Laura. *Perfection Salad: Women and Cooking at the Turn of the Century*, Farrar, Straus & Giroux, 1986.
Soyer, Alexis. *Délassements Culinaires*, 1845; *The Gastronomic Regenerator*, 1846; *The Poor Man's Regenerator*, 1847; *The Modern Housewife*, 1849; *The Pantropheon*, 1853, all Simpkin & Marshall. *Shilling Cookery for the People*, Routledge, 1854.
    A Culinary Campaign, Routledge, 1857.
Spain, Nancy. *Mrs. Beeton and Her Husband*, Collins, 1946.
Symons, Michael. *One Continuous Picnic: A History of Eating in Australia*, Duck Press, 1982.
Waterson, Merlin. *The Servant's Hall: A Domestic History of Erddig*, Routledge & Kegan Paul, 1980.
Wilson, C. Anne. *Food and Drink in Britain*, Constable, 1973; Penguin, 1976.
Wyvern (Colonel Arthur Robert Kenney Herbert). *Culinary Jottings for Madras*, Higginbotham, 1878.
    Fifty Breakfasts, 1894; *Fifty Dinners*, 1895; *Fifty Luncheons*, 1896, all Edward Arnold.
Yarwood, Doreen. *500 Years of Technology in the Home*, Batsford, 1983.

PARFAIT OF CHOCOLATE (TOP RIGHT) AND GATEAU DE PISTACHE

INDEX